A NEW SEASON

A Robertson Family Love Story of Brokenness and Redemption

AL & LISA
ROBERTSON

with Beth Clark

HOWARD BOOKS
A DIVISION OF SIMON & SCHUSTER, INC.

NEW YORK   NASHVILLE   LONDON   TORONTO   SYDNEY   NEW DELHI

Howard Books
A Division of Simon & Schuster, Inc.
1230 Avenue of the Americas
New York, NY 10020

First Howard Books hardcover edition January 2015

HOWARD and colophon are trademarks of Simon & Schuster, Inc.

For information about special discounts for bulk purchases, please contact Simon & Schuster Special Sales at 1-866-506-1949 or business@simonandschuster.com.

The Simon & Schuster Speakers Bureau can bring authors to your live event. For more information or to book an event, contact the Simon & Schuster Speakers Bureau at 1-866-248-3049 or visit our website at www.simonspeakers.com.

Interior design by Jaime Putorti
Jacket design by Bruce Gore
Front jacket photograph by Steven Palowsky
Back jacket photograph by Shutterstock

Manufactured in the United States of America

10 9 8 7 6 5 4 3 2 1

Library of Congress Cataloging-in-Publication Data

ISBN 978-1-4767-7320-9
ISBN 978-1-4767-7359-9 (ebook)

To Anna, Jay, Carley, Bailey,
Sage and Alex, Vinny and Corban.
You are the hope and the reason that
keep us going from season to season.
We will always love you.

Contents

CONTENTS

Acknowledgments

We want to first thank God, Jesus, and the Holy Spirit for their work in our lives every day and for guiding us through the past thirty years to our current season.

To our parents, thank you for raising us, loving us, and helping us all of these years; we literally wouldn't be here without you. Hoot, we miss you dearly and will see you again.

To Barbara and Ray, we wish there would have been more time with you. We miss you both terribly.

To Jason/Missy, Willie/Korie, Jep/Jessica, and all of our nephews and nieces, you make working fun and family will always come first.

To Aunt Ann, thanks for always being there for us and allowing us to be there for you.

To all the Robertson aunts and uncles, you shaped and guided us and were great examples to us.

To our WFR staff and friends, we miss you terribly, but all of those years together shaped us and got us ready for where we are now. You will always be our best buds.

To our fellow elders/wives at WFR, thank you for being such

great godly examples and for sharing the burden of helping shepherd the body of Christ.

To Carl Allison, Bill Smith, Ray Melton, Mike Kellett, and other mentors who taught us how to love ministry and love people when they weren't so lovable.

To those who financially supported us in the early days, the Howards, Owens, Tommy/K-K, and the Pine Street church in Vivian. Because of you, we were able to eat and survive.

To Howard Karbo, you have been there with us through every season. They don't make friends like you very often.

To the Idoms, Bill, Angelly, and Grace Burke for all of the laughter and all of the joy you have brought to us through the years.

To John and Paula Godwin and Laura Keegan, you guys were there when we needed you the most. Thanks for your friendship and for allowing us to be ourselves around you.

To Dianne Phillips, you were a light at our darkest point and guided us out of the wilderness. We will always be grateful.

To Joe and Alice Beam, because you shared your lives, we had a blueprint to survive.

To Randy and Joneal Kirby and Mac and Mary Owen, you asked us to serve and help marriages when we weren't sure what we had to offer. Thanks for having faith in us.

To Bill Phillips and Greg Eppinette, my childhood friends whom I could still call on when needed.

To our Duck Commander Family, we love working with you and appreciate your dedication to our family.

ACKNOWLEDGMENTS

To Jonathan Merkh, Philis Boultinghouse, Amanda Demastus, Jennifer Smith, and the crew at Howard Books, thanks for your skill and hard work.

To Mel and Margaret, Lee, Jessie, Deana, and the rest of our friends at WME, thanks for believing in this book and for what you do for us every day.

The Robertson Family

Al and Lisa may not always show up on television screens or find themselves in the spotlight as much as some other Robertsons, but they are an amazing behind-the-scenes presence in our family. In many ways, they're our anchor and our compass. In other words, they keep us grounded, and they help us know which way to go when we need guidance and godly direction.

Before *Duck Dynasty* became one of cable television's most popular shows ever, we were a relatively unknown group of duck call makers and wives in Louisiana. We faced the same hopes, dreams, and struggles as other American families. We still do. And when we run into challenges, Al and Lisa are the people we run to.

As a family, when we think of Al and Lisa, two words that come to mind for us are *admiration* and *appreciation*. We admire them for their strength of heart, their spiritual maturity, their character and integrity, their courage, their perseverance through difficulties, and their unbreakable, unending commitment to each other. We admire the way they love God, each other, and their family and for the way they use the lessons of their own brokenness to help others.

We appreciate the love, wisdom, and godly advice they provide for all of us as we navigate the seasons of our lives. We're grateful for the great role models they are for us and for our families. We appreciate them for loving us unconditionally and for being people we can trust and depend on, no matter what.

When we found out Al and Lisa were writing this book, we all wanted to share something personal about what they mean to us.

FROM PHIL AND KAY: We have tremendous love, respect, and admiration for Al and Lisa because of their strong, solid marriage (which has not come easily) and their Christian maturity, and because they are just such fun people to be with. When we think about who they are, all we have to do is look at the fruit of the Spirit in Galatians 5:22-23. That list of qualities describes them perfectly. Their lives always seem to exhibit love, joy, peace, long-suffering (which is like patience on steroids), kindness, goodness, gentleness, and self-control. That's who they are!

We are so thankful to have Al and Lisa in our family because they have a soothing, steadying effect on us all. They relate well to everyone—the older members of the family and the younger ones. Al and Lisa are the "go-to" couple when there are problems. As the oldest brother of four boys, Al is always available to help and counsel the men in our family, and they really look up to him. Lisa functions in the same way with the women in our family, and they admire her greatly.

They are well-versed in Scripture and they have served our home congregation and many other believers through Al's work as a pastor and elder and through the teaching and counseling they provide. They are exceptionally gifted at bringing peaceful solutions to crisis situations, whether the crisis pertains to our family, our church, or any of their many friends. No matter what people need, Al and Lisa are always there to help.

WILLIE AND KORIE: As the oldest brother and sister-in-law in this big, crazy Robertson family, Al and Lisa have been there for us in the good times and bad. They are a great example of a marriage that loves, forgives, and stays together through the tough times. Plus, they are the most fun people to be around. Their willingness to share their story is a testimony to their generosity of spirit; they really to want to help others through what they have been through. This is how they live their lives. You will enjoy getting to know Al and Lisa, but most importantly they will point you to the One who saved them.

JASE AND MISSY: When Jase and I (Missy) got married, I had only one sister-in-law. Lisa had been married to Al for a little more than five years, and they already had two baby girls. Al and Lisa had overcome some major struggles in their marriage by this time, and from what we could see, things seemed to be working out for them. Lisa was an encouragement to me as a new wife, and she mentored me in what being a Robertson was all about. A few years later, when the truth came out about Lisa's affair, I became witness to what unfaithfulness looks like in a family. Heartbroken and devastated, I saw how this selfish act was about to break up a beautiful family. I—and most everyone else—believed that this marriage had been damaged too badly to ever be put back together again. But because of Al's spirit of forgiveness, patience, and unwavering love for his wife and Lisa's sincere repentance, they began to rebuild what could have been lost forever. Only through their trust in God and complete sacrifice to His will were they able to accomplish this. Lisa has proven, without a shadow of a doubt, that her life is completely devoted to her Savior Jesus Christ. The old Lisa is gone, and the new is covered by the blood of Jesus.

What a blessing both she and Al are to our family! We are proud to call them our brother and sister, and we could not ask for better role models for our children. Their lives are open books, not because they are proud of what they have done in the past, but just the opposite. They are ashamed of their past deeds, just as we all are ashamed of our own sins. But they are willing to expose their failures in order to help others come to the same realization they have: that Jesus Christ can bring you back from the dead. We thank God for them!

JEP AND JESSICA: Al and Lisa have been key instruments in helping us learn how to build a God-centered marriage. Through Scripture and life lessons they have learned as individuals and as a couple, they have shown us how to build a lasting marriage. We are eternally grateful for their love for our Father, their love for each other, and their perseverance through all the struggles they have overcome. Because of their openness and honesty, many lives have and will continue be changed.

• • •

All of us know how powerful Al and Lisa's story is, because we know how powerful their lives are. We are excited about this book because we know their message of hope and redemption is life-changing. God bless you as you get to know Al and Lisa better and as you find hope, strength, and redemption through the pages of this book!

Introduction

Many people would look at the photo on the cover of this book and think, *That couple looks really happy.* They would be right. We're unbelievably happy. But we have not always been. Our life together is amazing, but we have had to fight for this amazing. As individuals and as a couple, we have walked through betrayal, abuse, abandonment, adultery, fear, shame, sadness, and loss. All those circumstances, and the brokenness they left in their wake, have now been redeemed in the most wonderful ways. We have seen God use each of those situations to teach us lessons we might not have learned any other way and to equip us to offer compassionate encouragement to others in similar circumstances. We have navigated lies and deceit and have emerged with the first-hand knowledge that truth really does set people free. We have endured pain we thought we could not bear and ended up in places of healing and strength we never dreamed possible.

Our life today overflows with joy. One of the best things about it is that we have had countless opportunities to share what we've learned with hurting couples—some on the brink of divorce. When couples come to us to talk about their failing marriages, they often say things like, "You won't believe what kind of trouble we're in," or "What one of us has done is so bad we're afraid you'll send us away when you hear about it."

We tend to respond by glancing at each other with a knowing look that says, "If they only knew what *we've* been through!" As we tell them about the mistakes we've made, they realize we have learned some lessons that may help their marriages have a happy ending instead of a tragic one. By the time we finish sharing our story, most people don't feel so bad about their own problems or negative behavior. Instead, they sense a spark of hope that gives them the courage to try to work things out, even if they have tried many times before.

We wrote this book to share a powerful message of hope, reconciliation, and redemption that rose up from the huge mess that was our marriage. We know from personal experience how miserable and broken individuals and relationships can be. We also know the depth and power of the redemption God can bring to situations that seem hopeless.

At this writing, we have thirty years of marriage and almost fifty years of living under our belts. One of the hallmarks of our lives and our relationship is *reconciliation*. Simply put, reconciliation is the idea that things and people that are broken can be put back together. What has been torn apart can be rejoined. On the back side of reconciliation, people often end up stronger, healthier, and wiser than they were before. Reconciled relationships tend to be more honest, more loving, and more committed than they were prior to falling apart. That's certainly what happened to us, and we know it can happen for anyone struggling in a difficult marriage today.

In our situation, we endured several kinds of brokenness, so we needed reconciliation on several levels. First and foremost, we both needed to be reconciled to God. We also needed to be reconciled to each other and to our family. No matter what people go through—whether it's addiction, rebellion (there's plenty of that in our story), marital problems, or some other type of broken relationship—the answer always begins with being reconciled to God. Once your relationship with Him is right, everything else eventually falls into place and healing begins. And one of the beautiful by-products of healing is the opportunity to help others find reconciliation in their lives. The apostle Paul writes in 2 Corinthians 5:18 that Christ "has given us the ministry of reconciliation." That's something we take seriously. We live lives that are reconciled to God and to each other, and now we share that reconciliation every chance we get.

> Reconciliation is the idea that things and people that are broken can be put back together.

We are honored that you have chosen to read this book. In it, we have been as honest and vulnerable as we know how to be. Parts of our story are intense and we write about them with transparency, hoping others who have been through similar situations will recognize us as fellow pilgrims on a journey that is not always pretty. At the end of each chapter, we take a couple of pages to look back and share the lessons we have learned through bad decisions or circumstances beyond our control.

Our prayer is that anyone caught in the same situations we

once faced will be able to learn from our experiences. We also hope that as a result of this book others will be able to avoid some of the disasters that nearly overcame us. Someone once said, "Experience is the best teacher," but we say that someone else's experience is a better teacher! We truly hope our experiences will help individuals and couples avoid some of the heartache we have endured.

Our message to you in the following pages is this: No matter what someone else has done to you or what you may have done to yourself, you can move beyond it. Nothing in your past has to keep you from an incredible future. Jesus says, "All things are possible," and He's talking to you. That means freedom from any bondage that has you entrapped. It means healing from any physical disease, mental condition, or emotional trauma that has had an impact on you. It means the ability to live in truth instead of feeling you have to continue to keep secrets. It means being able to hold your head high instead of feeling weighed down with shame all the time.

> Freedom means being able to hold your head high instead of feeling weighed down with shame all the time.

We want you to know that whatever you are going through right now, life can be good again. It won't happen overnight; it may take months or years of learning to live in wholeness one step at a time. But we are living proof that it *can* happen. We hope and pray our story will inspire you to believe that for yourself and give you the encouragement and practical advice you need to start walking in a new direction, toward a brand-new season of strength, blessing, and joy.

Chapter 1

THE BEARDLESS BROTHER

My frame was not hidden from You,
When I was made in secret . . .
Your eyes saw my substance, being yet unformed.
And in Your book they were all written,
The days fashioned for me,
When as yet there were none of them.

—PSALM 139:15–16

AL: People frequently associate the men of *Duck Dynasty* with long, bushy beards. My dad has one, my brothers all have one, and my uncle Si has one that is a little bit lopsided so it won't interfere with his shotgun. Not me. I'm often called the "Beardless Brother."

I have not been featured on our television show as much as my brothers have, especially Willie and Jase. My first significant appearance on our family's television show came when I had the honor of officiating my parents' vow renewal in the premiere of season four. I have heard that episode brought tears to the eyes of a lot of our fans, especially those aware of the hardships my parents endured during their early years of marriage. My mom definitely suffered, and from the time I was very young, I had an up-close and personal view of her struggles and her courage. I witnessed things no one else saw in those days in the late 1960s and early '70s. Maybe that's why leading my parents in that beautiful service by the river meant so much to me. Sure, being on television was fun, but standing before our family and friends and seeing my parents so in love and so committed after almost fifty years together—some wonderful years, some horrible—brought me true joy and happiness.

When I do appear on *Duck Dynasty*, I usually play the role of mediator, voice of reason, or go-to person when someone has a problem. Not much different from the way I function in our family in real life! At a young age, I found myself needing to shoulder a lot of responsibility, and as the big brother to three younger boys whose father was gone a lot, I became a leader in my family. With the exception of a season of foolishness and wild living, I have been a leader ever since. From time to time, though, I do still like to irritate my brothers for fun. Only an older brother can do that in love, right?

Having grown up as the son of the Duck Commander, I definitely know how to make a good duck call, and I enjoy being in a duck blind as much as the other men in my family. Though I am part of our family business now, I spent many years of my professional life in church work and ministry. That, and the fact that I'm clean shaven, sets me apart from my dad, my brothers, and Uncle Si in the minds of our audience. Those things have also made me a little mysterious, so in this chapter I want to give people a chance to get to know me, the Beardless Brother.

A LUMPY MONKEY

You may be aware that my mom, known as "Miss Kay," got pregnant with me before she and my dad, Phil, were married. My mom turned seventeen on December 21, 1964, while she and Dad were living in Ruston, Louisiana, where he attended Louisiana Tech University. I was born at Lincoln General Hospital in Ruston on January 5, 1965. I guess I could say that, at just a few days old, I made my media debut in a local newspaper photo with Mom because I was the first baby born in Lincoln parish that year. Obviously, if five days of the New Year passed before a baby was born in the parish, the population was not exactly booming.

Unfortunately, I was not what people consider a "beautiful baby." I had to fight to make my entrance into the world and was finally delivered by forceps, which made my head lumpy. In addition, the forceps slipped during my birth and hit my left eye. The eye did not open for three weeks! Mom was so young and inexperienced that she thought babies were like puppies—she didn't know my eyes were supposed to be open. All of this resulted in my uncle Tommy's giving me the nickname "Lumpy Monkey."

> Mom was so young and inexperienced that she thought babies were like puppies—she didn't know my eyes were supposed to be open.

Our young family spent a lot of time with Uncle Tommy and his wife during my first few years because he and my dad were both in college and Dad was a star quarterback. I will always respect my mom for finishing high school with a newborn and a husband who felt more comfortable in a duck blind or on a football field than changing diapers. My mom has written about this time in our lives in *The Women of Duck Commander*, and Dad wrote about it in *Happy, Happy, Happy*, so I will not go into detail. I will just say it was a very rough time for all of us. My dad was the way he was—which was very challenging to say the least—and my mom stuck it out.

JUNCTION CITY

When I was four years old, Dad graduated college and we moved to Junction City, Arkansas, where he took a job teaching and coaching at a school while working on his master's degree. Mom worked for the superintendent of the school system, and with both of my parents employed by the school district, we were able to live in a house on the school campus. Later that year, Jase was born.

In those days, in a small town in Arkansas, there was no such thing as day care or Mother's Day Out. My parents had to work, so they found someone to care for Jase and enrolled me in school. Even though I entered first grade at only four years old, I was somehow able to handle myself socially and academically with six-year-olds.

By the time I was in third grade, life was wonderful for me. We still lived on the school property, which meant the whole playground was available to me whenever I wanted to build forts, zip down a slide, or swing on the monkey bars. In addition, the nearby cemetery proved irresistible to me as an adventurous, imaginative, all-boy kind of kid. I do not remember ever being afraid of much. In fact, I was infatuated with fire and even jumped into a pile of smoldering debris in our local dump, burning both my feet. Apparently, I didn't learn my lesson, because on another occasion, I took a running leap into a pile of dry leaves—not realizing they were actually covering a lower layer of leaves that had been reduced to embers—and burned my feet *again*, resulting in major blisters for days.

We had no money for doctor bills in those days, so whether I had burned feet or one of my many cuts and bruises, Mom or Dad did the best they could with it. I'm sure Mom had a habit, like many mothers, of kissing things to make them better, and I remember Dad taking a needle and thread to stitch together some of my most gaping wounds. Things like that might be appalling to people today, but they characterized the way we lived.

BAD COMPANY, GOOD NEIGHBORS

During that time, Dad had some hunting buddies who were not good influences on him. He began to spend more time drinking and carousing with them and less time at home with us. So, of course, my parents' marriage became more difficult than it already was, and Dad became abusive. His abuse was mostly verbal, not often physical. I did get spanked on a regular basis, but I have to admit that I deserved most of those spankings.

As our family life deteriorated, I began to feel responsible for certain things. In a way, maybe I felt I had to be the man of the house because no one else was filling that role. I definitely cared about my mother and hated the way she was being treated, but she handled these less-than-ideal circumstances with great strength and courage. Mom was very aware of her need to work in those early days and help provide for our family. I think she learned early that she would always have to carry a heavier load than most women, as she tried to be there for her boys and work to make up for Dad's deficiencies. She had an inner strength and knew that she was able to be both parents when Dad wasn't around. She took care of Jase and me, but I also took on a caretaking role for Jase. Even at that young age, I understood intuitively that our family situation was bad, and something in me wanted to look out for my little brother.

I had no idea that someone—or Someone—had been looking out for me too. I now know that God had an amazing couple in place to help me after we moved onto the school property. Back then, I just thought they were nice neighbors. This preacher and his wife, Brother and Sister Layton, were probably in their seventies. They came to meet our family as soon as we moved in and quickly befriended me, almost adopting me as a grandchild. By that time, Sister Layton had been blind for about twelve years, but that did not stop her from making cookies and Kool-Aid for me almost every afternoon and telling me Bible stories while I snacked.

The first summer we lived in Junction City, Brother and Sister Layton took me to Vacation Bible School at their church, and I had a great time being with other children, playing, and learning about God. They also took me to church every Sunday and every Wednesday night. I had no idea then what a crucial time that was for me: the Laytons were laying a foundation that would sustain me for the rest of my life, as they helped me learn basic biblical principles, characters, and stories. They made it possible for me to have a meaningful connection with God and church, and I was the only person in my family who had any kind of spiritual relationship at all at that point. I look back now and realize that my mom has always had a tender heart for God, but during those years she was simply doing her best to survive. Since Dad would not go to church, she did not go either.

My dad has always had a great personality, and people in Junction City loved him because of it. But they also knew he was a drunk, and his reputation suffered. He held his job at the school for about three years, then quit when he realized he was about to be fired because of the way he was living. I do not know exactly what all was going on at that time, but I do remember asking him if he would take me hunting and he said, "No." When I wanted to know why, he told me he might have to take off running from the game warden. He meant it. He was doing some illegal things in his outdoor activities, but I did not understand that at the time.

Though I could not have articulated it, I did perceive that all he really wanted to do was hunt, fish, and drink and that having a family was a drain on his lifestyle. It was not a happy time.

NO PLACE TO RAISE A FAMILY

When Dad quit his job at the school, we had to move. He found work managing a bar outside Junction City, and we lived in a trailer next to the bar. This decision made a big statement to his Christian parents and siblings that he was committed to his lifestyle of drinking. By that time, Willie had come along, so all five of us—two parents, three-year-old Jase, newborn Willie, and me—lived in a one-bedroom trailer with a tiny living area and a kitchen so small we could hardly turn around in it.

> Dad got into a serious altercation, a real fracas, complete with ambulances and police cars, which resulted in his taking off into the woods running from the law.

Once we moved from the school property, the Laytons no longer came to pick me up for church. Thankfully, another lady from their church lived close to us and developed an interest in me. She started taking me to church, so I never lost my connection there, and I will always be grateful for that.

Within a year, we were able to expand our home to a fourteen-by-seventy-foot trailer, which made our living conditions more comfortable. Dad made good money at the bar, but the environment was not positive for our family. Mom never did like having us boys exposed to the things we saw around the bar—some very bad things—but she went along with it because the job provided a measure of financial security, and she did not know what else Dad could do because of his drinking.

After running the bar for a couple of years, Dad got into a fight with the owners. It was a serious altercation, a real fracas, complete with ambulances and police cars, which resulted in his taking off into the woods running from the law. That left my mom alone with three young boys. She ended up having to move quickly, taking us and basically just our clothes with her. Because the bar owners insisted she leave the state immediately, she had to leave her washing machine, dryer, and many of her mementos and special things in a storage shed. Mom and Dad had saved some money by that time, but she used it to pay off the bar owners and get us out of Arkansas. Our lives were about to get a lot worse.

SEASONED REFLECTIONS . . .

AL: When I look back at the difficult beginnings our family endured—from Mom's getting pregnant at sixteen to Dad's wild, irresponsible ways—I am grateful that God saw the big picture all along. He always knew those bad situations were temporary. He had complete confidence that He would lead us through, and eventually out of, the circumstances that threatened to destroy my dad as a person, my parents' marriage, and our life as a family. The enemy had a plan to ruin us, but God had a plan to save us, redeem us, and bless us.

> Even though my parents did not go to church, God reached out to all of us by reaching out to me through this couple.

I believe God was working in our family when we did not even know it. We had no clue when we moved to Junction City that the Laytons would be our neighbors and that God would use them to connect us to Himself. Even though my parents did not go to church, God reached out to all of us by reaching out to me through this couple. He had planted a seed of faith in our previous generations, but it was not deeply rooted or growing by the time I came along. So He watered and nourished that seed in me as a child. Over a period of years, that seed of faith took root and began to flourish in our family. Now our faith is the most important aspect of our lives, and all of us are walking with God—even my dad, who once seemed the least likely person in the world to become a Christian.

No matter what we were going through, God had a plan for our family. First and foremost, He had a plan that would eventually bring each of us into a personal relationship with Himself through His Son, Jesus Christ. Second Peter 3:9 says that God is not willing for anyone to perish, which means He wants to bring every person on earth into a personal relationship of salvation through His Son, Jesus Christ. That included my parents, my brothers, and me—and it includes you.

Eventually, God's big-picture plan for our family also included reconciliation between my parents, who now enjoy a wonderful, loving marriage. It involved great relationships among what is now a big extended family, as well as a position of influence through a television show—the last thing we could have ever imagined doing when we got kicked out of Arkansas.

Little did I know when we left Junction City that we would ultimately end up in West Monroe, Louisiana, a place where God would literally change our lives. Even though I faced hardships as a teenager—due to my own bad choices—and heartbreak as a young husband and father, I can say with conviction that God has been with me through every difficulty. Starting from the day I was born, God has turned the most bitter situations sweet. The journey has not been easy, but it has been rich and has now brought me to a place of happiness, peace, and the greatest love I've ever known.

When I think about what could have happened to my family and to me during those rough periods when I was young, I think about Romans 8:28: "We know that all things work together for good to those who love God, to those who are called according to His purpose." For sure, not everything we went through was "good." Some of it was very, very bad. But I can see now that God did work all of it together—using each experience as a part of a greater whole—to do something redemptive in our family.

If you or someone you love is going through a situation that seems hopeless, if things are so bad that it seems they can *never* be good—have hope. I am living proof that bad beginnings can lead to happy endings. God has a big picture in mind for your life, just as He did for my family and me all those years ago. Stay close to God, persevere through the hard times, and believe life can be better—and pretty soon it will be.

Chapter 2

A LITTLE BOY WITH BIG RESPONSIBILITIES

It is good for a man to bear the yoke in his youth.

—LAMENTATIONS 3:27

AL: With Dad hiding out in the woods, Mom moved the trailer and us boys to Farmerville, Louisiana, a little town about thirty miles from Junction City. The bar owners had specifically told her to leave the state of Arkansas, so we did, while still remaining fairly close to where we thought Dad was hiding out. From time to time, Mom would slip off to see Dad and bring him supplies and let him know how we were doing. But he never came out of the woods into town, and we kids didn't see him at all during that time. I am sure my parents communicated in some way, but I was never aware of any interaction between them.

At that time, understandably, my mom grew extremely discouraged. I watched her grow sadder and sadder as her life became more and more difficult. She felt abandoned and alone, and she was under tremendous pressure to support and care for three growing boys. Now that I'm an adult, I can see that she was simply trying to keep our family together and that she desperately wanted to matter to my dad. She reached a point where she no longer wanted to live the life she was dealing with. Mom writes about a particular moment during this season of her life in *The Women of Duck Commander*:

> *In the midst of that low place, the darkest place I have ever been emotionally, with thoughts of sleep and rest filling my mind, through my sobs I heard the scurry of little feet headed toward the bathroom door. I could tell all three boys, in their house shoes, were coming to talk to me. Alan spoke first: "Mom, don't cry. Don't cry anymore. God will take care of us." I was silent for a moment. Then I heard Jase ask, "Did she quit crying?" And I could hear Willie doing something he did often, making smacking noises while sucking on two of his fingers.*
>
> *I spoke to my sons through the door. "I'm okay. I love y'all. I'll be out in a minute."*
>
> *I then got on my knees and prayed, "God, help me. Just help me. I don't want to leave these kids. I don't know what to do or where to find You. Just lead me to somebody who can help me."**

I remember that day vividly. And I remember telling my mother God would take care of us. Though that was a tragic,

---

*   Kay, Korie, Missy, Jessica, and Lisa Robertson, *The Women of Duck Commander* (Nashville, TN: Howard Books, 2014), 99.

desperate moment, I can now talk about it lightheartedly and say it was my first sermon. When Mom said she was okay and came out of the bathroom, I knew my "sermon" had gotten a good response. Had I simply known to take up a collection, that moment could have been a sanctioned assembly!

Seriously, though, she now says that moment was her turnaround. That dark place was where she finally started searching for God. Over time God answered her prayers in amazing ways. Nothing remarkable or spectacular happened immediately, but our lives slowly began to change.

But things didn't get better right away; they only got worse. Dad eventually came out of the woods and joined us in the trailer in Farmerville. Dad had the skills to survive in the woods. He was great at living off the land. But once he came back to the trailer, he had to get a job, and that was a challenge for him. He finally went to work on an offshore oil platform—one week on and one week off. The job paid well, but it created an inconsistent family life because Dad was gone two weeks of every month. When he was home, he spent his time hunting, fishing, and drinking. He was in a full-blown downward spiral and none of us could do anything about it.

> Nothing remarkable or spectacular happened immediately, but our lives slowly began to change.

By this time, I was in about the fifth grade but still only eight or nine years old because I'd started school so early, and Jase was in kindergarten. Mom was working for Howard Brothers (Korie's grandfather's company) in West Monroe, about forty-five minutes from Farmerville. Every day, Jase and I rode the bus to and from school, and Willie, a toddler, stayed with a lady who ran a small day care.

I remember thinking, *Dad is gone all the time. Sometimes he comes home from work, but even when he's home he's not there. We have no dad, and our mom doesn't get home from work until six o'clock every night.* I was young, but I perceived the problems in our family accurately. I not only perceived them, I felt responsible for dealing with them.

Some people find this hard to believe, but I really did understand responsibility at eight years old. Mom worked and Dad was gone—either working, hunting, or fishing—so that left me to take care of Jase and Willie when school was out and when Willie was not in day care. Back then, people didn't worry about leaving children home alone the way they do today.

I had lots of chances to prove I was responsible, so my parents gave me a lot of freedom and trusted me with the younger boys. I fed them, bathed them, and made sure they were safe— including changing Willie's diapers! When Mom got home from work, I had often completed everything that needed to be done for the boys and all the housework. I cannot explain how or why I knew to behave this way at such a young age; I just did. That was the way life had to work for us at that time, and it did work. I never took much time to play back then because something always needed to be done and because I would never have left my brothers alone. I was their big brother, and I was going to make sure they were taken care of.

KICKED OUT

While we were living in Farmerville, Dad's lifestyle finally got so bad that he kicked Mom, my brothers, and me out of the trailer. He accused Mom of sneaking around with other men, which could not have been farther from the truth. She laughs about those accusations now and asks, "When in the world would I have had time to run around? I had a full-time job and three little boys!" In reality, Dad was the one running around, and his allegations against Mom were nothing more than projections of his own guilt. I think Mom understood that, but none of the rest of us did.

We left the trailer, sad and scared, and went to Dad's brother's house. He was afraid of Dad, so he only allowed us to stay one night in his home. We soon moved to West Monroe, Louisiana, to be closer to Mom's job.

Before we left Farmerville, Mom had started going to church and taking us boys with her. She knew she needed spiritual help, so once we were in West Monroe, she quickly turned to White's Ferry Road Church for assistance. Several people she knew from work, including her boss, Mr. Howard, attended that church, so looking to them for assistance made sense.

The church was amazing. Mom received the help, support, and guidance she needed—spiritually and on a practical level. People from the church even helped us get an apartment and extended generosity to us in many ways. We had nothing but our clothes and a suitcase at that point—no furniture, no dishes, no linens, nothing. The first time we knew Dad was offshore, we snuck back to the trailer in Farmerville to get some things we needed, but generally speaking, we had to leave almost everything behind and did not have much at all.

By that time, about 1975, Mom had decided she did not want Dad to know where we were because she was afraid of him. As months went by, we slowly built a new life without him. Mom had a good job, we were going to a great church, and people from the church were helping to meet our needs. I still took care of Willie and Jase and felt a lot of responsibility, but I was also very happy. Jase and I rode a big pink bus to church each week, not because Mom wouldn't take us, but because the bus—with its puppets and other activities for children—was so much fun. Even though we basically had nothing and our dad was not with us, life was going well for us.

Then Dad came back.

DAD'S HOME

Dad showed up in the parking lot of Mom's workplace one afternoon. She was afraid to approach him, not knowing what his condition might be. But when she walked up to his truck, she realized he was crying. "I want my family back," he told her, "and I am never going to drink again."

Mom told Dad that he could not stop drinking and change

his life all by himself. He finally admitted that he knew he needed God, and she believed he was telling the truth. Mom arranged for him to meet with a preacher that evening, and within a week, Dad had committed to following God and was baptized.

My brothers and I were excited to have our family back together. Dad did stop drinking very soon after he came home. He also began attending church with us and continued to study the Bible and grow in his faith. Even though he had lived a wayward lifestyle for a long time, several people in the church recognized his potential and realized that if he ever got his act together, he would be a powerful influence in God's Kingdom.

> Dad finally admitted that he knew he needed God, and Mom believed he was telling the truth.

A Christian school met in our church, and that's where I started sixth grade, after Christmas break, even though I was barely ten years old. Who was my homeroom teacher? My dad. Some of the leaders of the school were also part of our church, and they arranged a teaching and coaching job for Dad. I could not have been happier. I was in a good school getting a good education, but even better, I got to spend time with my dad every day.

In 1976, my parents moved to a piece of property on the Ouachita River, where they still live. I was in seventh grade, still riding to school each morning with Dad, and Jase rode with us. That's when my dad and I really began to build the relationship we still enjoy to this day. I listened to everything he had to say and watched his every move. I can still see his fingers tapping out the beat of his favorite songs on the radio, from Lynyrd Skynyrd to the Eagles.

By then Dad had reached a point where he wanted to share his faith with anyone who would listen, especially high school students. He practiced a lot on me, and that helped me grow and reconnect with the spiritual roots I had developed years earlier in Junction City. Whenever he taught people the Bible, I listened, when possible—I learned a lot from this man whose life was being totally transformed right before my eyes. That time in our lives was a tremendous bonding experience with him for me.

CAREER CHANGE

Dad was a great teacher and coach, but those things were not his life's passion. The only thing that did not change when he committed his life to Christ was his love for hunting and fishing. Prior to the summer of 1977, Dad had done some commercial fishing part-time, as his school schedule allowed, and had been making and selling duck calls. After school was out in 1977, he resigned his teaching and coaching job and dedicated himself full-time to commercial fishing and trying to get his duck call business off the ground. This was the end of my time at the Christian school and the end of spending so much of each school day with Dad, but I knew he would be happy with his new work.

I would have to go to public school the next year, having no idea I would meet a girl named Lisa there. We did not become friends immediately, but I will let her tell that part of the story. For now, I'll just say that I would have missed the greatest blessings of my life had Dad's job change not necessitated my move to a new school.

SEASONED REFLECTIONS . . .

AL: One of the great lessons I have learned over the course of my lifetime is that with God people can change. Some people get off to a difficult start in life or they hit a rough spot at some point on their life's journey and think the rest of their life is ruined. Because of something that has happened in the past, they do not believe they could possibly enjoy a great future. Two situations that happened in my life before I was even twelve years old have taught me to think differently about how the past impacts the future.

First, I sometimes look back on the responsibilities I carried as a boy and smile. While most boys my age were playing Little League ball or going to Cub Scout meetings, I was cooking, cleaning house, bathing brothers, and yes, changing Willie's diapers. Any time he gets a little "too big for his britches," as we say in the South, I remind him of that! I did not view any of those duties as hardship: I saw them almost as a matter of survival for my mom, my brothers, and me. But my mom now talks openly about the things I missed during childhood. She knows she could not have made it through that period of time without me, but she still regrets the opportunities I missed.

I really don't feel cheated out of my childhood, at least not in any way that God has not made up for. I'm glad I could help my mom through such a rough time. God has compensated for so many things I did not get to do as a child. I now have happy, healthy grandchildren who love to play, and I take time to have as much fun with them as their parents will allow. I have a great job that I thoroughly enjoy, I have an amazing marriage, and best of all, my whole family enjoys strong relationships with God and with each other.

People looking at me during certain seasons of my growing up could have easily thought I did not have a chance at a decent life. And had God not intervened in our family, and had we not allowed Him to intervene, I might not have. But God did intervene, and today I am living a life that, although not perfect, is better than anything I could have scripted for myself, even in my wildest dreams.

Second, I know the past does not have to dictate the future because I saw a complete transformation in my dad when I was a boy. From a young age, I have believed in God's ability to work miracles because I saw how thoroughly my dad changed once he gave his life to Christ.

Christianity was not an easy sell to my dad. He had never been a person who trusted others easily, so when the preacher came to our apartment to share the gospel with him, he asked a lot of hard questions. When he was not with the preacher, he studied Scripture for himself. He is not the kind of guy who would have committed himself to a radical life change without thoroughly investigating what he was getting himself into. Dad was a skeptic when he decided to listen to what the preacher had to say and to read the Bible for himself, but he was a *desperate* skeptic. Deep down, he knew he had made a mess of his life and of our family, and he reached a point where he truly wanted to change. God knew that. God saw his heart, saw his brokenness and his sincerity. And He turned a very messed-up man into one of the boldest, most devoted Christians I have ever known. Dad is certainly aware of his past, but he is not shackled to it. He's a living example of 2 Corinthians 5:17: "Therefore, if anyone is in Christ, he is a new creation; old things have passed away; behold, all things have become new."

No matter what has happened to you, what other people may have done to you, or what you have done to yourself, your past does not have to determine your future. If my dad can go from being a carousing drunk to being the man of God, the man of principle, and the man of courage he is today, *anybody* can change with God's help. If my family and I can go from living in a low-rent apartment with nothing but a suitcase to the level of blessings we now enjoy, any situation can turn around. Luke 1:37 says, "With God nothing will be impossible."

> Dad was a skeptic when he decided to listen to what the preacher had to say and to read the Bible for himself, but he was a *desperate* skeptic.

If something negative or painful has happened to you and caused you to think you cannot overcome it or move beyond it, be encouraged. Whether it affected your life twenty years ago or twenty minutes ago, God is willing and able to redeem the situation and heal you from its effects so you can move forward into a blessed life. He *still* has a great future ahead of you if you will follow Him as He leads you into it.

Chapter 3

A GIRL NAMED LISA

A bruised reed He will not break,

And smoking flax He will not quench;

He will bring forth justice for truth.

—ISAIAH 42:3

LISA: I was born and raised in West Monroe, Louisiana, where Al and I, and our children and grandchildren, still live. I am the youngest of three children and came into the world as a surprise to my parents, who thought they were finished having children. My parents were married for forty-eight years before my dad passed away in 2004. I was especially close to my dad, and one of my favorite memories is sitting in front of our big television watching the original *Hawaii Five-O* series with him every week. My dad was an amazing man. Everyone who knew him loved him. He never met a stranger, always wore a big smile, and loved to joke and laugh. His eyes were sky blue and as big as half dollars. My granddaughter Bailey has those eyes, and I am grateful God gave them to her; I can look into them and see my daddy.

My father was the best dad a little girl could ask for. He was my biggest fan, he could correct me with a smile, and he loved me unconditionally. His nickname was "Hoot," and the nickname he gave me was "Kid." When I was young, it was "Little Kid," but as I got older, it became just "Kid." I knew he meant *his* kid, and that gave me a strong sense of belonging.

My mother was married briefly before she married my dad. That marriage produced my brother, Harvey Ray Gibson (we called him "Ray"), and my dad adopted him as a toddler. My brother was twelve years older than I, and he left home when I was five years old to join the military and get married. I would definitely say my brother was a good big brother, but I barely knew him until he got out of the military and moved back to West Monroe with his small family.

I was very proud of my brother and of his being a Marine. I was seven years old when his first son was born, and I loved spending time with him; my sister-in-law, Diana; and their four children, Alif, Jimmy, Carla, and Harvey.

After my brother died, I stayed in touch with his children and their families, who all still live in West Monroe. I was so happy to be able to host our Christmas Eve get-together in 2013 at the new home Al and I had moved into earlier that year. I think that was the first time in about twelve years that we were all in the same house. They are my family, and I love them all very much.

My only sister, Barbara, was seven years older than I, and she was my idol. When I was young, I worshipped her and thought she was the coolest, most beautiful, most captivating person I had ever known. Plus, Barbara *always* had a boyfriend, and for reasons I will explain later, I thought that was great. At an early age I ended up being boy crazy too. My affection and admiration for Barbara never wavered, even though I knew better than anyone— because I slept in her bed each night—that she had a terrible problem with alcohol. I can remember lying in bed when Barbara came home drunk after being out with her boyfriend or a group of teenagers up to no good, hearing her and my mother yell and scream horrible things at each other. And I remember promising myself at that young age that I would *not* go down the same path. Though I could not have explained that commitment in a mature way as a little girl, I intentionally made a strong determination not to get involved with alcohol, not to have a string of men parading through my life, and not to end up fighting with people who loved me.

Now both my sister and brother are deceased, but I am thankful that my mother lives in West Monroe, along with all the Robertsons. I am surrounded by family, and I love it. I have not always loved my life, though, and I do not blame anyone for that. Some things happened that no one knew about, so no one did anything about them, and these experiences impacted me in negative ways for years. I have a sordid past, and I have no problem stating that fact. What's more important, though, is that I have a *redeemed* past—and that's something I share openly because I have learned that doing so helps and ministers to people who have been through similar traumatic circumstances. I'll write more about that later.

> Some things happened that no one knew about, so no one did anything about them, and these experiences impacted me in negative ways for years.

In spite of the challenges I faced growing up, I had a fairly "typical" childhood in many ways. We lived in the country and attended church together as a family. I was a Brownie and a Girl Scout, I played basketball, and I was a cheerleader. I wanted to be a part of everything and was active and involved in the things that interested me. I really enjoyed being around people my age and made friends easily. Everyone seemed to like me, and I liked them. But I also had a secret I could not share with them.

I HAD TO GO SOMEWHERE

As Al mentioned earlier, we did not have access to day care facilities when he and I were young the way people have access to them today. Most of the time, friends, neighbors, or family members took care of children who needed adult supervision. Just as Phil and Kay sent Al to school at age four so someone could look after him while they worked, my mother sent me to my grandmother's house while she and my dad were at work— five mornings a week during the school year and all day each weekday during summers and holidays. I have a lot of difficult memories of being at my grandmother's house, and a couple of good ones. The good ones are that she let me drink sweet tea for breakfast and she taught me how to garden and fish. The bad ones—well, they used to be my secret. Now they're part of my story.

My grandmother's name was Allie. I still love that name. I should have named one of my daughters Allie, but when they came along I already had a cousin named after our grandmother. My grandmother was a lot like Miss Kay in that she cooked three meals a day and served everyone who came into her home. She always cooked extra because someone always came by and was hungry.

My grandmother had long white hair that I think she washed a couple of times a week—the only times we ever saw it down. Otherwise, she wore it in a bun on her head. She was also "a full-figured lady," as we choose to call it, and my mom says I have her build on the backside! Yes, a little too much junk in the trunk.

My grandmother lived about five minutes from my mom's workplace in Bawcomville, Louisiana. About a block from her house, on a corner, was a store, and I loved to walk to the store for my grandmother to purchase her snuff. It was very powdery, not like the Copenhagen the Robertson men dip, and it came in a silver can.

My grandmother had an old coffee can that she spit in, and I remember one day when her friend Ms. Lizzie wanted to spit in it, but I wouldn't let her. My grandmother said, "Liser" (that's what she called me), "let my friend spit in that can."

I said, "She can get her own can. This one is yours. It's *gross* for her to spit in your can." She was so angry with me for saying that.

Ms. Lizzie did eventually get to spit in that can, but not because I shared it with her!

I have great memories of my grandmother as a person. I just do not have good memories of the times I was taken advantage of in her home.

THIS SHOULD NOT HAVE HAPPENED

My mother was one of eleven children (one who died as a child in a fire), and three of her brothers still lived at home off and on for most of the time I stayed with my grandmother. They were emotionally unpredictable and volatile; I never knew when shouting would erupt or when one of them would start throwing punches or waving a knife—or whether the police would show up. It was a frightening environment for a child.

The worst part of being at my grandmother's house was that one of my male relatives, who sometimes came to her house and who had severe drug and alcohol problems, molested me. My earliest memory of this abuse is when I was about seven years old. He did things that made me feel dirty, bad, and used, though the violations never involved intercourse. I don't remember exactly how he threatened me to keep me from telling anyone, but whatever he did worked. All I can think of is that he probably said my dad would be upset if he knew about it. I adored my dad, so I never told him. I just carried my shame and my secret. One morning I called my mother at work and begged her to come get me and take me home. I do not remember why that particular day was so bad or what gave me the courage (or desperation) to call her. I only remember that she did not come.

I never did bond well with my mother as I got older. Maybe because the darkness in me didn't feel deserving of a mother's bond. Or maybe it had to do with the harsh way my mother treated Barbara. I loved my sister, and seeing my mother so stern with her may have driven a wedge into my relationship with my mom. The older I got—especially as I moved into my teenage years and the darkness in me became more powerful—the more I clashed with her.

Barbara and my dad were the two people with whom I had close relationships, and Barbara moved out of our house as soon as she graduated high school. She moved in with a relative we knew would provide a safe environment for her because she could no longer stand the yelling and fighting that went on between my mother and her. They pushed all the wrong buttons in each other, which escalated the anger in both of them and drove them farther and farther apart until Barbara could not stand it anymore.

> The older I got—especially as I moved into my teenage years and the darkness in me became more powerful—the more I clashed with her.

Barbara's leaving was extremely hard on me. Not only was I alone without her to talk to, I also felt my hero and role model had left me behind. Because of my strained relationship with my mother and with Barbara gone, I had no one to talk to about what was happening to me, so I kept it to myself.

On the rare occasions I did see Barbara, I could never bring myself to tell her what was happening to me because I somehow thought it was my fault (that was another lie) and I did not want her to be angry with me or think I was responsible for it. She did not know about it until several months before she died. That's when I found out she had been abused too—by a preacher, she said. She told our mother about it, but Mom did not believe her.

Because I have now learned that I was not the only girl whom this man molested, I have wondered whether Barbara was abused by the same relative and she chose not to name him for some reason. On this earth, I will never know the truth about what happened to her. We did not have a chance to talk about it in detail, which is one of my biggest regrets. She needed to know it was not her fault and that she was not a bad person because of what happened to her too. I just waited too late to reveal my secret and learn about hers.

The abuse continued until I was about fourteen years old. My grandfather died that year, and when all of our family was at my grandparents' house for his funeral, this horrible man found me alone. I still cannot believe he even considered molesting me during the funeral activities!

That day, I had had enough. I finally stood up for myself and said, "If you ever touch me again, I will tell my dad. And *he will kill you*." To this day, I am absolutely positive I was right about that.

My abuser never sought me out after that. My father died without ever knowing what had happened to me. I did not men-tion it to my mother after I called her to come get me that day because I didn't think she would believe me. Once I had grandchildren, I did tell her about the relative who molested because there were times she kept them and he came around her house, so I wanted to make sure they were protected.

So that's a big part of the story of my early years. A somewhat typical beginning gone bad because of a selfish, lustful man—and no one to talk to about it. A beautiful hero of a sister who silently suffered the same things I did and dealt with them in negative ways that no one understood. Two girls, seven years apart in age, both excessively boy crazy for deep, dark, shameful reasons. And, as I will write about in the next chapter, a good-looking boy who caught my attention in the sixth grade and changed my life.

SEASONED REFLECTIONS . . .

LISA: I first shared my story of abuse with national and international audiences in the book *The Women of Duck Commander* and was overwhelmed by the large number of women who contacted me to say that they too had been sexually abused and to thank me for being bold enough to go public with such an intimate story. Somehow, knowing about my journey helped them feel less alone and gave them courage to believe they could heal, and that has made my choice to bring a very painful, very personal situation out into the open worth making.

When a news website featured the abuse aspect of my story, one reader commented that he thought I shared about the abuse as an excuse for bad decisions I made as an adult, which I will write about later in this book. My response to that is this: Things happen to people. Sometimes those things are very bad and they do great damage, to the point of influencing a person's life in the most negative ways for years after they take place. The fact is, those things often become the root systems of future choices and behaviors. Generally speaking, they are not excuses; they are reasons. They don't justify bad choices. Instead, they explain why people are often unable to make good decisions.

As a child, while the abuse was taking place, and as a teenager, after I confronted my abuser, I never had a chance to get the help I needed. I was not old enough to understand how traumatic it was emotionally and mentally or how devastating it would be to my future relationships. The lingering effects of the abuse would haunt me for years because I did not know how to deal with them or where to turn for help.

The things that happen to us—especially things that have powerful emotional consequences such as fear or shame—don't just go away, nor does their influence on our thoughts and behavior diminish as we get older. No, the things that happen to us matter; they can affect us for the rest of our lives, sometimes severely. In the wake of trauma such as sexual abuse or other incidents, people often lose or confuse their sense of purpose. When people have been deeply hurt, they may be able to function on some level, but they end up dysfunctional in other ways. Eventually, those unhealed wounds in the soul lead them to do something that makes them wonder, *How did I end up like this?* They do things they don't understand, and often, because their traumas are shrouded in secrecy, people close to them don't understand either. They feel a distance between themselves and other people and between themselves and God—and they cannot figure out why. The isolation and alienation they feel gets worse and worse. I first learned these things because I lived them and because I watched my sister die from them—in a way—on August 17, 2008.

> The fact is, bad things that happen to us often become the root systems of future choices and behaviors.

I am now 100 percent convinced that my sister's drinking problems began with the sexual abuse she suffered. Some people may have thought she was just "wild," but that was not the whole truth. Barbara drank because she had been violated at a young age and did not know how to process what had happened to her. She did not know how to cope with it or how to begin to heal, but she could not live with the pain of it, so she used alcohol as a means of relief and escape.

The tragic difference between Barbara and me is that she died before she had a chance to be healed. The impact of her past ultimately led her to a battle with alcoholism that she could not win. I still miss her and long to share my healing with her.

Barbara's daughter, Whitnee, now has three daughters with her husband, Paul Bass, and they live in West Monroe. I am thankful that they live near us and that we can see each other as often as we do. Barbara also had a son, Logan, who passed away on September 28, 2008, after a motorcycle accident. Barbara's husband, Bill Wilson, and his wife, Carol, live in Alabama, and I stay in touch with them as much as possible.

My life has turned out differently from Barbara's, thanks to the grace of God. It's also turned out differently because of a cute boy I met when I was in the sixth grade, a guy I will write about in the next chapter and love for the rest of my life. He and his family have loved me in the most amazing ways, and that has been vital to the healing and restoration God has brought to me.

Today, I am thankful that the wall of shame so many abuse victims feel they must hide behind is coming down. Churches now offer programs to help people heal, and entire ministries are devoted to helping people find redemption from the very things Barbara and I—and maybe even you—have endured. I urge you: If you have suffered any kind of trauma, especially as a child, get help from a qualified, credentialed therapist or minister. Don't pretend it didn't happen anymore. The journey to healing is not easy, but it's worth it—and it can happen in your life.

Chapter 4

MR. PINECREST

Keep your heart with all diligence,
For out of it spring the issues of life.

—PROVERBS 4:23

LISA: A couple of years before I confronted the man who molested me, I started sixth grade at Pinecrest Elementary and Junior High School in West Monroe. That's where I first caught a glimpse of the cutest boy I had ever seen. He was in eighth grade, which meant that he was part of the cool, older group of students, while I was just a lowly sixth grader. I could hardly take my eyes off him, but he never noticed me. As Al says today, "I was too busy strutting my stuff and wearing my leisure suits!"

When I say Al was cute, I mean really, *really* good-looking. Pretty much everyone thought so. Even though he was new to the school as an eighth grader, his handsome looks and great personality caught the other students' attention, especially the girls—and the other boys did *not* like that. During that year, he was even voted "Mr. Pinecrest," which was supposed to mean he embodied the values of our school but actually meant he personified the values all the girls thought were important! Basically, being Mr. Pinecrest meant he was the most popular guy in the school.

I had more than a little preteen crush on Al. I really wanted him to be my boyfriend, even though I was only about twelve years old. The reason for this is that the best role model I had in my life at that time was Barbara. Like a lot of little girls, I could not envision being my mother's age—and at age twelve, I did not really want to be—but I could easily envision myself as a teenager like Barbara, and that whole idea was very appealing to me. Barbara wore makeup, Barbara smoked cigarettes, and Barbara had boyfriends. I knew I couldn't get out of the house with makeup on my face, and my sister took all the cigarette butts my parents had smoked, but there was no reason I could not have a boyfriend. And I could not imagine anyone better than Al Robertson. I guess I've always believed in aiming high!

> **Every morning when I went to school, I could hardly wait for an Al sighting.**

Every morning when I went to school, I could hardly wait for an Al sighting. Every lunch break, recess, or fire drill, I was on the lookout for him. I saw him often but felt invisible. He didn't even look at me, much less say hello, in those early days.

I thought my sixth-grade heart would break at the end of the year when Al moved on to high school and I knew I would have to finish my last two years at Pinecrest without him. Thankfully, other Robertsons came along, and I became friends with Jase and Willie (Willie's classmates at Pinecrest knew him as Jess).

That meant Al visited the school occasionally, and when he did, I always seemed to be watching.

A WHOLE NEW WORLD

AL: Even though I was vaguely aware of Lisa during my eighth-grade year at Pinecrest, she is right when she says I did not pay any attention to her. During that year I was enjoying myself, aware that I was very popular, having fun with my friends, and hanging around with an eighth-grade girl I considered my girlfriend. When our time at Pinecrest ended, though, so did my relationship with her. I had definitely started noticing and liking girls by this point in my life, but I was not interested in that blond-haired sixth grader, even though she was much closer to my age than the girls in my grade. If I could cut it with older girls, I figured that was what I wanted to do.

I spent my ninth-grade year at a new school, and that's when things began to take a downward turn for me spiritually. Until that point, I had held firmly to my faith. Because of the Laytons, I had spiritual roots and a relationship with God. Even though my family life had been hard, I had a good church experience. I was having a great time at White's Ferry Road Church, and by then all of our family attended church together and both my parents were Christians—as were Dad's parents, who lived in a little house next to us on the river.

I also turned thirteen that year, and puberty hit hard. I became more interested than ever in girls, especially pretty, well-developed ones. Like a lot of high school freshmen, I started going to football games on weekends, though I did not pay much attention to what was happening on the field because there were so many girls to meet and talk to. On weekdays, I discovered kissing girls in the back of the school bus, though I never tried much more than that. Even though I was a Christian, I became much more interested in things of the flesh than things of the Spirit.

I faced the challenge of being only thirteen but also being in ninth grade, which meant my peers were doing things I had not done before and probably was not ready for emotionally. Where girls and relationships were concerned, I became aware of things before I should have known about them. As a young boy I had seen people having sex behind the bar my dad managed (this is part of what I meant when I wrote about being exposed to bad things I shouldn't have seen). So I was definitely curious, but I did not act on my curiosity. I had plenty of friends, I was still a responsible person, and I made straight A's. People thought of me as a "good kid," but I was beginning to stray from my personal values as a believer and from what my family expected of me.

MY FIRST GIRLFRIEND

I had my first serious girlfriend when I was in tenth grade, yet I was only fourteen years old. She was sixteen. I knew her during my ninth-grade year but really noticed her when school started in 1979. When she climbed onto the school bus that fall—well, all I can say is that the summer had been kind to her. She had expanded in all the right places, as far as a hormone-filled young man was concerned. I went from attraction to lust in about ten seconds.

I could hardly believe my good luck when this girl agreed to start dating me. After all, a two-year age difference is significant at fourteen and sixteen. I pretty much felt like the king of the world, or at least the coolest person on earth. I still went to church but had basically lost my interest in spiritual things. I was not nearly as concerned about pleasing God as I was about pleasing an "older woman." At the same time, though, I still wanted to be "a good Christian." I was living a double life—my "church life" and the other parts of my life. I wanted to do right—but I didn't want to stop doing wrong. I was a teenage boy, and I was enjoying the worldly experiences I was having.

My family life was strong at this time. Mom, Dad, Granny, Pa, my brothers, and I all ate dinner together every night, played games, and generally had a great time. I had good Christian role models in my parents and grandparents, and my brothers were active in church and doing their best to live Christlike lives, even though they were young. I had everything I needed to help me be a godly young man, and part of me wanted to live that way. But another part of me didn't, and that part won the battle.

At sixteen, my girlfriend already had a car, and I was barely old enough to get a learner's permit! I became sexually active for the first time in that car, and that put me on a dangerous path that would not end for years. For most of my tenth-grade year and part of my eleventh-grade year, we had sex frequently, usually at her house, after school, when her parents were not home. I am, of course, ashamed of my behavior now, but at the time, I felt like one lucky fourteen-year-old.

No More Mr. Pinecrest

After I turned fifteen, I got a new girlfriend, but I was involved with her in the same ways I was involved with the previous one. One of the biggest events of that year was that I was able to get my driver's license, which opened a whole new world to me. I was free to go where I wanted to go, and that's when my drinking and carousing, even trying marijuana, started. I could have had some good friends from church, but in my young mind, church people did not have any fun. I decided instead to hang around with guys I thought I could have "fun" with, two of whom were Lisa's cousins, but really all we did was get into trouble.

My parents knew I was going to church and they thought I was behaving, even though I was not. I don't know whether they were in denial about my lifestyle, whether they were so busy building the Duck Commander business that they didn't notice, or whether because I'd always been such a good, responsible son it never occurred to them that I might stray. I do know they had no idea how I was really living. The few times they did question me about something, I lied, and probably because they had always been able to trust me, they believed me. I would have been in *big* trouble, especially with Dad, had they been aware of what I was doing. Their good boy had gone wild.

SEASONED REFLECTIONS . . .

LISA: Some people think a sixth grader with the level of infatuation I had for Al is perfectly normal, or at least acceptable. Others would call it "precocious." In my case, it was not normal because it was rooted in the abuse I had suffered. I call it "the 'why' behind my 'what.'" In other words, it was the driving force behind behavior some people might have considered inappropriate. At the time, I'm sure people thought I was simply trying to imitate Barbara, or at least taking my cues from her, and on some level that is true. On a deeper level, though, the abuse not only violated my body, it messed with my mind. It planted a lie in my thought process—the lie that I existed to please men.

I knew I did not want to please older, creepy men like my abuser. That idea was repulsive. But unconsciously I think I felt I was supposed to have a "man" in my life to please. I cannot remember whether my relative said something to cause me to think this way or whether my messed-up perceptions of myself and my purpose simply grew out of being used inappropriately. I do know that the abuse directly affected my self-esteem and my view of who I was and how I was supposed to live—in the most negative and damaging ways. On a practical level, it made me obsessed with Mr. Pinecrest—

> The abuse I'd suffered planted a lie in my thought process—the lie that I existed to please men.

though once he left our school, I was not aware of how he was living.

If I could gather a group of boy-crazy preteen and young teenage girls today, I would give them the best advice I know, advice that no one gave me but that would have helped me so much and perhaps enabled me to avoid some costly mistakes through my tumultuous teen years. I would encourage them to hold tight to the gift that God gave them. A young person's virginity is a precious and valuable gift. Once given away, it cannot be recaptured.

I would also let them know that the gift of their bodies should only be given to someone who has pledged a lifelong commitment before God and their family and friends in marriage. If purity has already been lost, I would tell them to recommit their lives and bodies to Christ and wait for their wedding day to exercise their union with someone. Waiting for the wedding day is best, which is why God instructs us to reserve sex for marriage. That way, the sexual experience is shared with one person and not multiple people. People who wait do not have the memories, shame, or guilt that are associated with premarital sex.

Whether you have walked in purity all your life or already engaged in sexual activity outside of marriage, I encourage you from this moment on to allow God to give you His strength to withstand other temptations until that blessed day.

AL: When I think back to my high school days, I have to shake my head at how arrogant I was. I really did think I was too cool for school, and one of the main reasons was that I could keep up with older guys, especially in the area of sexuality. Over the years, as I have studied and learned about God's plan for intimacy, I see that in my quest to be impressive, I failed God—and myself—miserably. I knew good Christian people were supposed to wait until marriage to have sex, but I could not imagine how anyone could actually do that. Beyond that, though, I also did not realize God has a divine design for intimacy and sexuality and I did not understand how vital following His plan is to healthy relationships.

God states His plan for marriage—the only appropriate intimate relationship for a man and a woman—in Genesis 2:24–25: "Therefore a man shall leave his father and mother and be joined to his wife, and they shall become one flesh. And they were both naked, the man and his wife, and were not ashamed." For years, I have preached and taught marriage classes based on four key principles in these verses: "leaving and cleaving" (which I call "severance"), unity, permanence, and then intimacy. Intimacy too often gets confused with the sexual act but actually includes emotional and spiritual closeness as much or more than physical intimacy. My problem as a young man was that I was old enough to want to have sex but not nearly old enough or mature enough to do anything God has designed to precede and surround a sexual relationship. In other words, I wanted the benefits and rewards without the responsibilities and commitments.

I know people think I am seriously old-fashioned, out-dated, irrelevant, out of touch, and maybe even crazy for believing and saying that sex belongs only in the context of the marriage relationship. And yes, I know that every-body is doing it—so to speak. Trust me, I know about hormones and prom nights and fraternity houses and business trips. I know all of that. But I believe something greater. I believe God's plan is best and I *believe* His Word is true. Lisa and I know from firsthand experience how dev-astating sexual relationships outside of marriage—both premarital sex and adultery—can be. We also know how great a physical relationship can be when it takes place within God's design.

Lisa and I realize that many people, for various reasons, engage in sex at young ages. We do not view that with even the slightest bit of condemnation or judgment. We simply want people to know that God's way is best and that anyone who wants to live a life of sexual purity can start right now—no matter what is in their past.

We're also aware that sometimes people look for a loop-hole in God's will for sexuality and make comments such as, "We don't want to wait until we're married. We need to find out if we're sexually compatible." The fact is, men and women are designed to be compatible. The idea of experimenting "to see if it will work" is nothing more than an excuse for sin. Lisa and I both have a history of sexual sin. (Which means we're familiar with all the reasons and excuses for not fol-lowing God's plan. Been there. Done that.) But we also have a history of forgiveness and redemption, and we know that no matter who you are or what you've done, new beginnings are always an option.

You can't keep doing the wrong thing and expect the right results. Make the right choice, follow the right path, change to the right course, and your life will reflect something wonderfully right and bright for your future.

Chapter 5

A ROCKY START

*Anyone who listens to the word but does not do what
it says is like someone who looks at his face in a
mirror and, after looking at himself, goes away and
immediately forgets what he looks like.*

—JAMES 1:23–24, NIV

AL: When my senior year in high school started in the fall of
1981, I only needed four credit hours to graduate, so I did not
have to go to school full-time. I went to school half a day each
weekday, and to fill the rest of my time and make some money, I
got a job sacking groceries at a Big Star supermarket and another
job hauling hay. My job at Big Star did not last long because I did
things like cut the bottoms out of egg boxes so all the eggs would
fall on the floor when the manager picked them up. And I don't
think it helped much that I also tumbled through the ceiling one
day when I ventured into an off-limits area upstairs and landed
on the meat counter between the ground beef and the pot roasts.

In spite of all my antics and the bad choices I made, I remained
a good student. I kept my grades up even when everything else

in my life was plummeting down. The worst thing about being sixteen and a senior was the attitude that came along with it. I thought I was a *stud*, and I wanted everyone to know it.

In those days, hanging out at McDonald's was a cool thing for teenagers to do. Of course, since I was *so* cool (in my own mind), I spent a lot of time under the golden arches. We leaned against our cars in the parking lot, with radios blaring, just kind of talking with each other. I did a lot of that in my senior year. One day, a gorgeous blonde caught my attention—and she can pick up the story from this point.

FINALLY!

LISA: I was so excited to go to high school, partly because I thought being in high school was cool, but mostly because I knew Al would be at the same school, and I could hardly wait to see him again. As a tenth grader, I would be the "new kid" and he would be a senior, but that did not matter to me.

I did not realize when school started that year that Al was no longer the "Mr. Nice Guy" I knew from Pinecrest. His life had taken a negative turn during his high school years, and he was hanging out with my cousin, drinking and smoking pot. I had felt a connection to him for several years by this time, and I did not let his new way of life affect my infatuation. He had a girlfriend during his senior year, though, so once again, he was oblivious to me.

Every weekend during the school year and most nights during the summer, the McDonald's parking lot in our town was full of teenagers. I went to McDonald's one night in that fall of 1981 and it finally happened: Al noticed me in line behind him at the drive-through. He got out of the car, walked up to my window, and asked, "What are you doing?"

All I could say was, "Waiting on you."

Right then and there, he asked me out on a date for the following Friday night. I was *so* excited! My dream was coming true!

> I went to McDonald's one night in that fall of 1981 and it finally happened: Al noticed me.

When he talks about that moment in the drive-through line, he says he noticed me because I had really grown up since my days as an awkward middle school stalker. He thought I was a "babe," and that's why he asked me out.

Over the next several days, I could hardly wait for the weekend. Al had asked me to meet him in West Monroe, and I thought maybe that was because both of us lived several miles outside of town. I wished he had offered to pick me up but tried not to let those bad manners bother me. I was too happy simply to be going out with him.

THIS WAS *NOT* WHAT I EXPECTED

When I arrived at the place where I was supposed to meet Al, I felt like someone had dumped a bucket of ice water on my head.

He was not alone! Two of my cousins were with him. I could hardly believe it. Who wants to go on a date with their cousins tagging along?

My cousins were just as wild as Al. None of them was a good influence on the others. I knew how my cousins were living, so having them along on the date did nothing to make me feel protected. They were an unwelcome part of this night I had looked forward to for so long, and I felt a little self-conscious because I thought they were influencing Al in the worst ways. Like most young girls, I just wanted to be alone with my date. I didn't want an audience.

The "date" was terrible. It consisted of the four of us riding around in a car while the guys drank and smoked pot. One of my cousins drove and the other sat in the passenger seat. Al and I sat in the backseat. I'll just say that he was accustomed to backseats, but I was not. Having my cousins in the car and being in the backseat with a guy for the first time made me feel terribly awkward. After all, I was only fifteen years old.

When driving around ceased to be fun for my cousins, they headed for a strip club. My two cousins went inside, creating the perfect opportunity for Al to start making out with me, and I went along with it. Pretty soon, Al passed out in the car, and I just sat there beside him, deeply disappointed, angry, uneasy about the whole evening, and feeling very unsafe in the parking lot of a strip club. For years, I had thought Al was a nice guy—maybe even a gentleman. That night, he proved me wrong. But I was still crazy about him.

FROM BAD TO WORSE

When Al talks about this time in our lives, he says that people would think our relationship could only get better after such a bad start. He knows he made a bad first impression and says he really thought he was a stud. But the truth is, things between us only got worse.

I was a "good girl"—and a virgin—when Al and I started dating. I had seen how alcohol affected my sister, but other than that I had not been around much drinking or any drug use (with the exception of some of my extended family who came around my grandmother's house when I was little). Al was eager to be my teacher, so over the next month or so I began drinking and smoking with him.

I really cared about Al, and he knew it. He could tell I was willing to do anything to please him. He acknowledges now that he pushed me to take our relationship to "the next level," using the classic line "If you love me, you'll give yourself fully to me."

He also admits he did not love me at all; he just wanted me in a physical way, and I lost my virginity to him when I was in tenth grade. Of course, he had no idea how my abuser had treated me and how that abuse had affected me. He did not realize how vulnerable I was or that saying no to him would have been almost impossible for me. I had been strong enough to tell off a grown man when I confronted the man who molested me after my grandfather's funeral just a few months earlier, but I had a weak spot for Al. I was willing, even eager, to do whatever he wanted to do.

Not only was I head-over-heels crazy for Al, I was also building a good relationship with his family. Soon after we started dating, he introduced me to his parents, grandparents, and brothers. We began spending time at their house—not a lot, because Al was still hiding his lifestyle from them, but we were around them enough for me to know that I really liked them and felt comfortable with them.

Al admits he did not love me at all; he just wanted me in a physical way, and I lost my virginity to him when I was in tenth grade.

That spring and summer, I thought I was in heaven! I was finally dating the man I had loved since sixth grade. I knew the way our relationship was going was not the way love was supposed to go, but who was I to say what love was really "supposed" to be like? We were physically intimate, and I was convinced we would be "in love" forever—and Al seemed content to let me believe that. I dreamed of dating him until I finished high school, then marrying him and living happily ever after. But Al had other plans.

MOVIN' ON

AL: I should have known my bad behavior would catch up with me, but like most teenage boys, I never even thought about that possibility. One day, a friend's mother called my mom to say she did not think I was a good influence on him and she did not want the two of us hanging around together anymore. This was major because almost everyone viewed him as one of the wildest guys in town. People would have thought *he* was a bad influence on *me*. When Miss Kay heard what his mother said, she had to pay attention, even though she had always respected me and thought highly of me. I am sure that the thought that I might be a trouble-maker was extremely hard on her, but my mom has always been one to face and deal with the truth when confronted with it.

Things got worse for me when my old girlfriend's father drove his pickup truck up to talk to my parents and me about a plumb-ing issue at his house. He was furious! I wasn't home at the time, but I heard about it loud and clear after I got home. His plumber had blamed the clogged pipes on all the condoms that had been flushed down the toilet while my girlfriend and I were dating. Instead of manning up and admitting to my parents that the con-doms were mine, I basically said, "Yeah, that girl sure does sleep around. Can you believe all those condoms in the pipes? I mean, the reason I broke up with her is that she was sleeping with so many guys." That was not true, but I was afraid of her father and afraid of what my own father would do if he found out I really was responsible for that problem. So I lied, and I think my par-ents believed me at the time. Once again, I was willing to trash someone else's reputation to make myself look better. What a self-ish creep!

These two big incidents happened along with other seem-ingly minor offenses involving things like drinking, smoking pot, wrecking cars, disrespecting people's property, and other bad behavior. At this point, I was my father's son: I could see the writing on the wall. Just as Dad quit his first teaching job in Junction City when he realized he was about to be fired over his drinking and carousing, I also saw that I was about to be in serious trouble. Not only did I see it, the Duck Commander himself and Miss Kay finally realized the truth about the way I was living and laid down the law. I could no longer live in their house and continue my lifestyle. I would have to shape up and abide by their rules, or I would have to move out. I finally told the truth about the way I was living, but I also chose to leave so I could continue living on my own terms.

SEASONED REFLECTIONS . . .

AL: My late teens were not my finest hour. I look back on that time in my life and am ashamed of the way I treated people, especially Lisa and my parents. I was not respectful toward Lisa and I continually deceived and lied to my parents. In addition, I was no longer a good role model for my brothers, who had grown up being able to trust and depend on me. I still feel especially bad about the way I treated Jase during that time. He was the oldest of my younger brothers and could see through my deceit, so I bullied him to shut him up. That's no way to treat a brother who is trying to help you, but the evil in my life had blinded me to his good intentions.

Both of my parents have written in their books that Jase was ultimately the one who told them how I was living. There came a point at which he refused to let them continue to give me the benefit of the doubt. My behavior was a crisis in our family, and Jase is the one who forced all of us to face it. I was furious and resentful at the time, but now I am so grateful to him for loving me enough to do everything he could do to pull me out of a destructive lifestyle, even though it meant I had to leave home.

When I think back about that season of my life, I think one event sums it up better than anything else—my fall through the ceiling at the grocery store. That happened because I was in an area clearly marked off-limits. In my rebellion, like a lot of teenagers, I wanted to do exactly what I was not supposed to do. I was not respectful of the rules of the store, and I simply was not wise. Thankfully, I did not get hurt as a result of that incident, but I did end up embarrassed and in a mess of raw meat. That's what happens when a person is foolish—he gets messed up!

Proverbs 9:10 says, "The fear of the Lord is the beginning of wisdom." No matter what you have done in your life, no matter how foolish you have been or how many stupid mistakes you have made (and I made plenty!), every day is a new opportunity to choose to be wise and to live in wisdom for the rest of your life.

LISA: One of the biggest problems I have ever had was the fact that I did not simply have a normal teenage crush on Al; I really did worship him. I gave him priority over everything and everyone else in my life. I loved him more than I loved anyone else, and I basically existed to please him. He was not domineering or demanding, so I cannot say he intimidated me into thinking I had to please him, but I wanted so desperately to be loved and to be with him that I said yes to anything I thought would make him happy—cigarettes, alcohol, recreational drugs, and sex. In my desperation to please him, I basically went from a "good girl" to a wild child in a matter of a few months after I started dating him. I did not have the strength or even the desire to uphold my own standards. When I look back at those early days with Al—starting with me as a starry-eyed sixth grader dreaming of my Prince Charming all the way through to our deeply disappointing first date years later—I can hardly believe the range of feelings I went through. Talk about a roller coaster of emotions! I know being in love—whether it's puppy love or the real thing—does funny things to a girl's heart. Where Al was concerned, my heart was like a thoroughbred, running after him at full speed with all its might, blind to the things going on around me, determined to win the prize. From the age of twelve to the age of fifteen, I was basically obsessed with Al. I adored him way too much, and that was not healthy or good for either one of us.

As Al and I have counseled couples and individuals through the years, we have found that women who have been abused by men either hate men or adore them and feel excessively needy toward them. If they adore men, they are never able to truly have an intimate, healthy relationship with a man because their adoration keeps them from relating to men as normal human beings. They view men as perfect (though no one is perfect), almost as gods, and then get their hearts broken when these men do something to disappoint them—usually something that would not be a huge problem in a healthy relationship. Many of these women go through men almost the way people flip through a magazine.

I was basically obsessed with Al. I adored him way too much, and that was not healthy or good for either one of us.

If women hate men as a result of abuse, they may end up in same-sex relationships, or they become embittered toward men in general, including their own husbands, if they get married. Alan and I have counseled some couples where the wife holds back love for her husband because she feels that he will take advantage of her, the way she was taken advantage of as a child. Either way, these women end up emotionally incapable of developing or maintaining the kind of relationship God intended for a man and a woman to have. I was definitely one who adored men, specifically one young man, Al. In years to come, that adoration would prove detrimental to me and hurtful to him, and almost destroyed our relationship.

Al and I can look back now, after thirty years of marriage, with absolute conviction that we were always meant to be together. We believe God would have led us into marriage at some point, with or without our painful history as teenagers. Though, of course, we ultimately ended up with each other, we did not get off to a good start, and we could have grown our relationship in a much better way. Had we built our relationship on a solid foundation, we most likely would have avoided much of the heartache we have endured. Not everyone realizes the drama we faced before we got married, so we'll tell that part of our story in the next chapter.

Chapter 6

LIFE SPINS OUT OF CONTROL

There is a way that seems right to a man,

But its end is the way of death.

—PROVERBS 14:12

AL: Given the way I was living, New Orleans seemed like an ideal place for me to find myself after I left home. My dad's sister Aunt Judy and her family lived in a bedroom community just outside New Orleans, and she agreed to let me stay with them for a while. She was the director of nursing at one of the hospitals in New Orleans and offered to find me a job. The whole arrangement seemed good to me, and I was eager to leave my West Monroe past behind for a new start in New Orleans. I'm sure my leaving broke my parents' hearts, but they were committed to tough love and to letting me make my own mistakes.

My parents were not the only ones whose hearts were broken when I decided to move away. Lisa was devastated. I was seventeen by this time and eager to prove myself in a big, happening city. Lisa, however, was only fifteen; she had just started dating the man of her dreams (me), and she was in love. She was convinced our relationship could stand the long-distance test; frankly, I didn't care whether it did or not. At that time, I was dating Lisa because I thought she was pretty, I knew she was a nice girl, and she was sleeping with me. I did not reciprocate the deep feelings she had toward me, nor did I share her commitment to our relationship. I told her that, yes, we were so in love we could definitely make a long-distance romance work. That was a lie and I knew it; I fully intended to be in hot pursuit of all the good-looking women I could find once I moved away. The most tragic part of my lie was that Lisa trusted me, so she believed what I told her.

> The most tragic part of my lie was that Lisa trusted me, so she believed what I told her.

Aunt Judy did get me a job in the same hospital where she worked, as a courier for the nurses. My responsibilities consisted of carrying documents, charts, lab reports, medications, supplies, and other things back and forth among the nurses and hospital employees. I thought I was the best-looking, most charismatic man in the universe. At seventeen, I was exceedingly flirtatious, I was arrogant, and I thought I was God's gift to women.

Most of the nurses were in their early to midtwenties. I told them I was twenty-one and spent my entire eight-hour shift complimenting and teasing them. I worked the night shift, eleven P.M. to seven A.M., which meant less supervision and more freedom than I would have had working days. I could not imagine a better job.

NOT A GREAT HOST

Back in West Monroe, my family missed me and Lisa was miserable without me. One weekend, my mom, brothers, and grandparents came to New Orleans, saying they wanted to visit Aunt Judy and Uncle Jim. They brought Lisa with them. I'll let her tell this part of the story from her perspective in the next chapter, but suffice it to say here that I did not treat her or my family well.

When they arrived, I was not even home. I was out on a date! In fact, the whole time they were in New Orleans, for several days, I showed up to see them only once. Lisa was shocked and heartbroken.

I did not realize for quite some time how much I had hurt her in so many ways—not picking her up when we went out but asking her to meet me, never having any money to even buy her a hamburger, introducing her to alcohol, allowing her to be around people who were smoking pot (including me), not respecting her feelings for me, pressing her to go faster and farther physically than we should have, robbing her of her virginity, and just generally taking advantage of her before flippantly saying, "I'm leaving," and basically abandoning her. I did talk to her by phone a few times from New Orleans, but once I left West Monroe, I was ready to dump my fifteen-year-old girlfriend for some "real women."

At the time, I could not have accurately described the way I treated her or put truthful labels on my bad actions. Lisa could not articulate everything I did to her either; she just knew she was devastated, and she cried all the way back to West Monroe and for a week afterward.

A CLOSE CALL

Before long, my life almost became one wild party after another in between my shifts at the hospital. I acted like I enjoyed the drinking and carousing because I thought it made me seem cool, but I really found it uncomfortable. I also went through two or three one-night stands but found them unsatisfying. Even then, something in me understood that sex is about intimacy and a relationship. I'm not sure how I knew that, but I believed a physical relationship needed to take place in the context of some level of exclusivity. Maybe that was because I saw such a powerful example of ironclad commitment in my mom during difficult times in her life. Maybe it was just part of my emotional makeup, or maybe I was a bit old-fashioned. Whatever the reason, I have always had a "commitment chip" in my relational wiring, so I quickly lost interest in sex for the sake of sex and focused on developing a steady relationship.

I could not have made a worse choice for this "steady relationship"—a twenty-six-year-old neonatal nurse who told me she was married but separated. She confided in me about all the struggles she faced in her marriage and about how unhappy she was and what terrible problems she had with her husband. Before long, she and I were sleeping together.

Something deep inside me kept whispering to me that what I was doing was not right. I was not ever completely comfortable with that relationship, and I never understood why she wanted to be so secretive and sly about it, but I stayed in it.

Once again, I was living a double life. I had become a master of disguise. Everyone around me seemed to love me because I had a great personality, but in reality I was not lovable at all. I was a self-serving, arrogant young man trying to act much older than my age. I was sleeping with a woman who was not my wife, and I was drinking more than ever and taking speed in order to be able to work at night without having to sleep away all my daylight hours. Where drugs were concerned, I feared getting caught with them and going to jail, so I definitely was not a "pothead" or anything like that, and I viewed speed as something I needed to keep me awake during the graveyard shift. I never had marijuana in my possession (even when I smoked it in my younger days) but rarely turned down a joint when someone offered me one. All the while, I kept my job, did the laundry at Aunt Judy's, cooked for the family, and cleaned their house. I never lost my sense of responsibility toward family, but I took no responsibility at all for my personal life, and I made one bad decision after another with my nurse girlfriend. That almost cost me my life.

THE WRONG END OF A CROWBAR

One Sunday morning, after I had been in New Orleans a little more than a year, I went to the nurse's apartment to tell her I could not see her anymore. For some reason I had begun to sense danger around us, and I realized she might have more of a story than I realized. Something about the relationship just did not feel safe, so I wanted to end it. As it turned out, I never got the courage to break up with her that day and ended up leaving her apartment without saying what I went there to say.

I had not driven my white 1976 Monte Carlo very far before two tires went flat. A man pulled over close to me, got out of his car, and asked about the tires. I could tell he was not interested in helping. Suddenly, he picked up my crowbar and began beating me with it, shouting profanities. I tried to wrestle it out of his hands and then took off running as fast as I could, barely escaping the crowbar when he hurled it at me. He was my girlfriend's husband.

I skidded into a convenience store, breathless and terrified, and told the clerk to call the police. I don't know how much time passed before they arrived, but it seemed like forever.

I got into the car with one of the police officers, who said he would take me back to my car. He asked, "Where's the gun?"

I did not know what he meant. Later, I guessed that he was testing me to see what I would say—he wanted to know who the gun belonged to.

As it turned out, after the assailant threw the crowbar, he ransacked my unlocked car and found a loaded gun. My uncle had given me the gun to carry for protection, and I had hidden it under the seat and forgotten about it. In his rage, my girlfriend's husband had used the gun to smash the glass on my car before he headed down the street after me. I'm sure he was intent on shooting me if he found me.

When the first police car arrived on the scene, my girlfriend's husband ran back to the car and threw the gun into it, through one of the broken windows. The police later removed the gun and placed it on the hood of my car

Suddenly, the guy picked up my crowbar and began beating me with it, shouting profanities.

with the chamber open for me to identify. Had I not run so fast, I feel certain I could have been shot to death. The guy was *that* angry.

When we got back to my car, a small crowd had gathered, including my girlfriend and several of her neighbors. Some of the neighbors had called the police before I did, and that's probably what kept my girlfriend's husband from following me to the convenience store and killing me in the candy aisle. Needless to say, my girlfriend was upset, more about the fact that I had lied to her about my age than anything else. The relationship ended up being over that day after all. I had to admit that my time in the Big Easy was not nearly as easy as I imagined it would be.

"Go Home"

After the chaos subsided and almost everyone had left the crime scene, I sat down on the curb, exhausted, dazed, and relieved to be alive. I realized the man who attacked me would not face any consequences for his behavior because he had a good relationship with the police as a drug informant. The police basically told me nothing was going to happen to him and that I should not have been running around with a married man's wife to begin with. I couldn't argue with that!

Eventually, the only person left besides me was the crime scene photographer. When he finished taking pictures, he walked over and sat down beside me. I don't remember word for word what he said, but he started asking me what I was doing and where I was from. He started talking about my family "back home," and I began to cry. He could tell I was a lost soul in a bad place, and he knew exactly the right things to say to me in that moment. The photographer ended the conversation by encouraging me to go home. When I look back on that moment, I realize that this man provided me with the way out of my mess. "Go to the hospital and turn in your resignation. Then go home. Get back to your family. You don't need to be here. If you keep living like this, something really bad is going to happen."

When I speak publicly, people often ask me if this man was an angel. I don't know. All I know is that from a biblical perspective, angels do function as God's messengers—and this man definitely had a message from God for me. I don't get caught up in who he was; I'm just thankful he talked to me that day.

After everything that had happened in New Orleans, I finally did want to go home. I did not want to run anymore, but I had no idea how my family would respond to my return. I started by going back to Aunt Judy's, bruised and beaten, and telling her and my uncle everything that had happened. They were shocked. After all, I'd been a model houseguest, even cooking and cleaning, and a reliable employee at the hospital. They had no idea what I had been doing on my off hours. "I am a mess," I told them. "I just need to go home."

> Dad was indeed standing in the driveway, but instead of yelling at me, he simply said, "We've been waiting for you."

They agreed wholeheartedly and helped me get ready to leave.

After being in New Orleans for about a year and a half, I called my mother and told her I was coming. All she said was, "Okay." I was nervous all the way back to West Monroe, hoping my dad would not be standing in the driveway ready to bawl me out when I got there and read me a list of rules I would have to obey in order to stay.

Dad was indeed standing in the driveway, but instead of yelling at me, he simply said, "We've been waiting for you." Then he invited me to go build some duck calls with him. Over the next few weeks, I started college, worked for Dad, and listened to him as he taught me the Bible. A couple of months after my return from New Orleans, I committed my life to Christ again, for all the right reasons, and Dad baptized me in the river by our house.

SEASONED REFLECTIONS . . .

AL: I cannot overemphasize the truth of the Bible verse at the beginning of this chapter: "There is a way that seems right to a man, but its end is the way of death" (Proverbs 14:12). So many people, including me in my younger days, think they know what is best for themselves. If they're anything like I was, they become arrogant and get impatient with the process of growing up, and they decide to take their lives into their own hands. This is usually not a good decision, but sometimes it turns out to be a positive learning experience, as it did for me.

When I decided to go home, I knew my parents had every reason to be furious with me. I was hoping my mother's tender heart and relief over having me home would keep her from being too angry. But I did not know exactly what to expect from my dad. I have said jokingly many times, "Making Phil Robertson mad is a very bad idea—as good a shot as he is!" I knew my dad had changed dramatically since the days before he entered into a personal relationship with Jesus Christ. His conversion resulted in his becoming a much more patient and emotionally disciplined man than he had been when he was younger. But I was also pretty sure I had crossed a line with him because of my actions before I left home and because of the trouble I got into in New Orleans. I hoped he would recognize my brokenness and go easy on me, but I was not counting on it.

When I got out of the car and heard him say, "We've been waiting for you. Let's go build some duck calls," I was not only relieved, I also felt I had encountered the purest, most genuine, godly love a person could ever experience. The way Dad dealt with me that day and in the following weeks and months changed my life—and our relationship—forever.

Sometimes I wonder if Dad remembered what rebellion was like and understood me better than I understood myself. In a way, my wild times were not much different from his. I did not have a wife or family to support, and I did not have to run from the law, but all forms of rebellion have a lot in common. I believe there was something in him that understood something in me. I am also convinced he knew I could change, because he had changed.

Lots of teenagers rebel in one way or another. Some forms of rebellion are fairly harmless while others can jeopardize a person's well-being or hopes for the future. As in my case, rebellion can threaten a young person's life. I'm sure a lot of parents are reading this book, and if you are the parent of a wayward son or daughter, I want to encourage you in four specific ways.

First, keep your own faith strong. Dealing with rebellion can be scary, frustrating, and exhausting. Only God can give you the strength and wisdom you need. Wayward children need someplace to come back to, and even though they seem not to respect your commitment to truth, trust me—as a prodigal son myself, I needed my parents to believe in something when I couldn't. I have looked back with a lot of godly pride because my parents loved God enough and loved me enough to confront me, challenge me, and ultimately release me to make my own faith decision. Had they simply allowed me to make a mockery of our family by openly living in rebellion without consequence, I would never have come to the ultimate decision to surrender my life to Christ. A strong faith that loves enough to maintain commitment and allow grace for wayward children to come home is the ultimate recipe for success when a family battles with a rebellious teen.

Second, if you have a spouse, keep your marriage vibrant. Don't let a stressful situation with one of your children drive a wedge between you and your partner. Even if the two of you disagree on how to handle it, focus on the areas of your life where you do agree. Rebellion and wild living can be a serious problem in a family, but don't let it consume your marriage. Find ways to nurture intimacy and even have fun together in the midst of this trial. A strong relationship with our spouses is essential, so we can rely on them when we become unsure of our own resolve.

Third, keep loving. No matter how much I hurt my family and Lisa, they never stopped loving me. When I pulled into the driveway at Mom and Dad's house by the river and saw my dad standing there waiting for me with no anger or judgment, I knew he loved me. When I realized how glad he was to have me home after all the trouble I'd gotten into, I knew everything would be all right. Rebellious young people are often deeply afraid and sometimes ashamed of their behavior once they realize what they've done. When they can also recognize how much they're loved, they have a much easier time changing their ways and learning to make good decisions.

Fourth, forgive and go on. Today, when I interact with my parents, my brothers, Lisa, and anyone else affected by my behavior as a young man, they do not act as though they are still hurt by what I did years ago. They have forgiven me completely, and they no longer hold my bad decisions against me. Sometimes we are told to "forgive and forget," but since forgetting is almost impossible, I like to say, "Forgive and move forward." In our family, everyone I hurt now treats me as though I never caused them any pain. This is one of the main reasons we have such strong relationships and such a great time together now. People in families are going to hurt each other, but if we will truly forgive, then everyone can move forward and enjoy good relationships. It may take a while, but it *can* happen.

> When I realized how glad Dad was to have me home after all the trouble I'd gotten into, I knew everything would be all right.

Chapter 7

FREE FALL

"When an impure spirit comes out of a person, it goes through arid places seeking rest and does not find it. Then it says, 'I will return to the house I left.' When it arrives, it finds the house swept clean and put in order. Then it goes and takes seven other spirits more wicked than itself, and they go in and live there. And the final condition of that person is worse than the first."

—LUKE 11:24–26, NIV 2011

LISA: As Al mentioned in the previous chapter, I traveled to New Orleans one weekend with his family. They said they wanted to visit Judy and Jim, and that made sense to me. At the time, though, I was not very interested in a visit with the extended family. I just wanted to see Al.

When we pulled up to Judy and Jim's house, I could hardly contain my excitement. I did not understand why Al had become more and more difficult to reach by phone over the previous weeks, but I was about to find out. He knew we were coming to visit, and when we arrived, he was on a date with someone else. That was his way of breaking up with me. When he and I speak publicly now about how God has redeemed and restored our relationship, Al admits he had no plans to continue dating me once he moved to New Orleans and that he did not have enough character or integrity to inform me of that decision. That hurt me more than anything I had experienced in my life to that point.

I COULD NOT HANDLE IT

After the trip to New Orleans, my broken heart sent me into a complete free fall. Before Al left for New Orleans, we had talked about the possibility of a long-distance relationship. I really did believe him when he said he thought we could do that. Besides, I believed that our physical intimacy would keep him loyal to me.

Until that point in my life, my experience with men other than my father or my brother was basically limited to the man who molested me. I knew that as long as I was available to him in inappropriate ways, he paid attention to me. I think, subconsciously, I expected Al to respond the same way. As long as I was willing to maintain a sexual relationship with him, I reasoned, he would still be my boyfriend. After all, I told myself, he really was a great guy.

Was I ever wrong! Al turned out to be everything I thought he was not. In some ways, I began to view him as I viewed the man who abused me—as nothing more than a user. In other ways, even though I was furious with him, I could not let go of him.

Clearly, he was trying to push me out of his life, but I could not get him out of my heart. As I struggled with my feelings for him, I made a blanket judgment against all males, deciding that they were only out to get whatever they could take from women and girls. I went through a season of completely giving up on the whole idea of love and never wanting to be involved with a guy again. But that did not last long.

For the next year and a half, I was a complete wreck. Most of that time, Al was still in New Orleans, but even after he came home, it was months before I heard from him. I was so devastated that I made one bad decision after another. I had little support from the people around me, and my mother said, "I told you so," because she never really liked Al anyway. That only made matters worse, because even though I was angry with Al, I could not stand to hear anyone say anything negative about him. I had been so infatuated with him for so long that I could not just erase him from my mind. By then, I had been interested in him for three or four years and we had been involved in an intimate relationship; I could not simply pretend none of that had happened. I had been through many experiences I thought were positive with him, and in spite of the fact that he hurt me, I was not willing to start believing the worst about him, even though I had plenty of reasons to do so. My thoughts and feelings were very complicated. I did not understand them, so I just continued to wrestle with them.

I was powerless to do anything about the mess I was in, so I said to myself, "I am so messed up and miserable that I'll just see how many other people I can mess up too." Seething with anger and disappointment, I was determined to make others miserable too.

When school started that fall, I skipped classes often and did poorly when I did go. In a frantic effort to find a substitute for my love for Al, I sought fulfillment in drinking to the point of passing out, having sex with anyone available, and chasing guys who seemed out of my reach. Though I am not proud of any of this now, I told myself at that time, "To hell with everything. I'll just get satisfaction wherever I can." I was driven and desperate, with no shame and no fear in my pursuit of guys. In fact, I even ended up in fights with other girls because I slept with their boyfriends. If I wanted a certain young man and knew he was involved with another girl, I went after him with greater intensity, as though the challenge made the conquest sweeter. I was in terrible shape, doing great damage to myself and to other people.

> Seething with anger and disappointment, I was determined to make others miserable too.

I believe now that my biggest problem at that time was thinking I knew what love was, when I did not really know anything about it at all. I had a gaping hole in my heart, and it cried out to be filled. I thought the way to meet that need was through relationships with guys. In fact, I dated people I did not even like, just to feel like I had a boyfriend, even if the relationship only lasted a week or so. Many times, as soon as a relationship got started, I wanted out of it. I could tell the person I was with was not going to meet my needs; that deep longing in my heart still was not satisfied. I did not know that Christ is the only one who offers perfect love or that only He could fill the emptiness inside me. I certainly did not know what healthy, mature Christian love between a man and a woman—even a young man and a young woman—was supposed to look like. Without that knowledge, I simply kept going from one guy to the next, looking for someone to make me feel significant. No one could do that, of course, because people are not made to function that way. Only God can heal a heart and give a person a sense of worth and value. Only He can lead people into healthy relationships and lay a foundation of true love in a person so all other relationships can be healthy too.

I Could Not Deal with Reality

When spring of my junior year in high school rolled around, most of the girls turned their attention to the prom—what they would wear and, more importantly, who their date would be. I hated the thought of the prom!

One of my friends had been involved with the same boyfriend since ninth grade. She was in love with him and talked a lot about their plans for prom. I could not bear to admit to myself or to anyone else that I did not have a date, so I lied and told everyone Al was coming back to West Monroe for the weekend to take me to the dance. I so desperately wanted that to be true that I almost believed it, but I knew intellectually that no such thing was going to happen. I had not even spoken to Al in months.

I wanted people to think someone cared about me the way my friend's boyfriend cared about her. I knew Al was not interested in me at that time, but I didn't want anyone else to know. My sense of self-worth was so destroyed by then that I had no capacity to be honest with others about my life or about the pain that was raging in my heart.

I was not living in a fantasy world where Al was concerned. I was well aware of his feelings—or lack of feelings—for me. I just decided to lie to other people about the relationship. When the time came to go to the prom, I made up an excuse for why Al could not come, and I invited someone else at the last minute.

This was an absolutely horrible time in my life. I never consciously considered suicide, but I did do things like getting drunk and then getting behind the wheel of a car. More times than I can count, I remember waking up in my car, in a field, with no idea where I was, how I got there, or who was in the passenger seat next to me. I thank God now for His amazing protection, which kept me safe and prevented me from hurting anyone else.

TRYING TO MOVE ON

At some point during those miserable, out-of-control days, I reached a time where the idea of having a steady boyfriend was more attractive than simply sleeping with one guy after another. In my heart, I knew no one would ever take Al's place, but I decided to try to find someone who could serve as a consolation prize. A friend introduced me to her cousin—who was about six years older than I was—and we started dating. He acted as though he really cared about me, and that was important to me. For a while, I thought maybe I had "found someone." My parents knew this young man's family and thought they were nice people, so they basically thought my relationship with him was acceptable despite our age difference. But it wasn't. I wish now that someone had tried to stop me from getting involved with him, but I know that had anyone interfered, I would have only clung to him more tightly. I was so rebellious and still so hurt over Al that no one could tell me anything; I was totally deaf to good advice.

My new boyfriend was old enough to buy alcohol and drugs, and at the time, I viewed that as a plus. Now that I had an "older man," I reasoned, I had a new supplier of all the things Al once provided me with, including sex.

I DIDN'T THINK I HAD A CHOICE

My boyfriend and I had been dating about nine months when I found out I was pregnant, several weeks before my seventeenth birthday. He was *so* excited; I was not. In fact, I was frightened, confused, and burdened by the whole situation.

"What am I going to do with a baby?" I asked myself, knowing I was completely unprepared for motherhood. But my biggest concern of all, and the question that ran through my mind nonstop, was, "What will Al think if he finds out about this?"

Even though he had clearly broken up with me, I never got over him. No matter how many other guys came and went in my life, including my boyfriend at the time, I continued to hold out hope that Al would someday come back to me. If I had a baby, I reasoned, there was *no chance* that would ever happen.

The dominant message about abortion in those days was the same one we hear today: "A fetus is not a baby. It is just a glob of tissue." I believed that message. After all, I was only sixteen. I was mature enough in my actions to get myself into that situation but not mature enough in my thinking to consider ways to get out of it. Besides, the people who told me it was just a glob of tissue were doctors and nurses. I trusted them with medical matters, never considering that they might be wrong.

> No matter how many other guys came and went in my life, I continued to hold out hope that Al would someday come back to me.

So I decided the only thing I could do was to abort it. I had no idea what I was doing and never thought about the consequences of my decision. I look back on those days now and can hardly believe how I processed the events of that time. The darkness in my life was overwhelming.

My boyfriend was furious with me for choosing to have an abortion. He loved me—at least he said he did—and wanted to marry me, even though I was not even seventeen. He wanted us to have our baby, but I could not do it. I did not love him; I still loved Al, and I was not willing to do anything that might keep him from choosing to resume our relationship.

Even though my boyfriend was angry about my decision, he

was also extremely concerned about me—so much so that he sent his mother to the doctor's office with me. After I went through with the abortion, everything was over between him and me. Despite the fact that he claimed to love me, I could not stand to be anywhere near him because he reminded me of what I had done.

NEXT . . .

Not too far from where Al and I now live is a billboard that has a picture of a little girl on it. Under that photo are the words *Kill her now and it's murder*. Next to the picture of the girl is a photo of a fetus, with the words *Kill her now and it's abortion*. I like that sign, in a painful kind of way, because it clearly connects abortion with the taking of a human life. I am sure that is one reason the repercussions of abortion are so devastating for so many women.

The abortion was more traumatic for me than I ever thought it would be. Anyone who tells a pregnant woman she can just get rid of a fetus and move on is dead wrong. Abortion is much more than a physical procedure; it is a major life decision with severe emotional consequences that often last for years and years. I still think about that time in my life—not every day, but fairly often—and wonder how I could have possibly even considered taking someone else's life. I have to remind myself that I simply did not see it in those terms when I was a teenager. All I could think about was what a burden it would be to my life and the fact that if I married the baby's father and that relationship did not work out, Al would not even think about reconnecting with me. I was so messed up!

In the weeks after the procedure, I laid low. For the first time in a long time, my level of interest in guys decreased. I equated guys with sex, and now I equated sex with pregnancy, and I did not want anything to do with that.

A few months later, the familiar ache in my heart began to resurface. I hated the aloneness of my life; I wanted to be with someone. I soon started dating a guy who lived down the road from me. He had a really cool car and I was impressed with that, but I remember little else about him. We dated for about eight months, but I did not have a physical relationship with him. I could not take that chance again.

He seemed to really like me and even mentioned marriage. I liked him, too, and for a while I went along with talking about the possibility of marriage. But in the end I did not like him *that* much. I still had high hopes of Al's coming back into my life as my Prince Charming and sweeping me off my feet. I had no reason to believe that would happen. In fact, at the time I had every reason to believe it would not. But that did not keep me from hoping.

SEASONED REFLECTIONS . . .

LISA: What a mess I was after Al broke up with me in such a passive, nonconfrontational way. I was faced with the truth that he was no longer interested when he didn't show up to see me when I visited New Orleans with his family. I now realize that my devastation was so severe because, as I mentioned before, I worshipped Al. I didn't just lose my boyfriend. I lost my god, and I could not deal with that. I felt empty, aimless, and completely void of any purpose in life.

I had no idea that I could have used that time in my life to step back, look for God, and discover my own sense of identity. All I knew was that I had lost the one person who mattered most to me. The emptiness inside me seemed to scream nonstop for something to fill it. The only way I knew to satisfy that longing was to find another guy.

I know now that the gaping, aching hole inside of me could only have been filled through a relationship with God. Had I chosen to pursue Him, I would have been spared much heartache in my own life and wouldn't have brought such heartache to the lives of people I loved. Unfortunately, I did not make that choice. As I will explain in later chapters, I did not enter into a life-changing relationship with God until I went through at least two more situations in which I made bad decisions that caused pain for me and for the people around me.

When I look back now at those months and years after

Al and I broke up, one of my biggest regrets is not seeking God's help when I was so upset over losing him. Another huge regret is not learning to forgive myself sooner for the abortion. I suffered over it for years, haunted with feelings of guilt and shame I could not shake, no matter how hard I tried.

I cannot overemphasize the importance of learning to forgive yourself for the things that pile guilt and condemnation on you. Whether it's an abortion, an addiction, a way in which you have hurt or damaged another person, or something else, the only way to move beyond it is to forgive yourself. Otherwise, you will stay trapped in negative feelings and you may even sabotage the blessings or successes that seem possible in your life.

I have spent time with many young women who have been molested, had abortions, and been through other types of trauma and shame. Lots of them tell me they simply cannot get over what happened to them. Without sounding harsh, I try to help them realize that saying they cannot move beyond it is the same as saying that Jesus did not do enough for them, that something about His death on the cross is insufficient. And that's just not true. His work at Calvary is more than adequate to heal anything we have done to ourselves or that anyone has done to us.

I often ask people who struggle to forgive themselves, "If Jesus can forgive you, why can't you forgive yourself?" That usually makes people think. I will do anything in my power to help people forgive themselves because I know we cannot live as victims. If we want to enjoy our lives, have great relationships, and fulfill the great purposes we are created for, we have to live victoriously in Christ. This is not always easy, and most of the time it's a long journey—sometimes two steps forward and three steps backward—but it's worth it.

I am living proof that people can forgive themselves. It's pretty much impossible in one's human strength, but once a person is in a relationship with Jesus Christ, the grace to forgive is available. I like to tell people they can always come home to Christ.

> Saying we cannot move beyond something is the same as saying that Jesus did not do enough for us, that something about His death on the cross is insufficient.

No matter what you have done, He is big enough to heal it. You can do a lot that's bad (and trust me, I know about this firsthand), but you can't do anything so bad that He will turn His back on you if you are genuinely sorry and ask for His help and forgiveness. His love completely overwhelms any mistake, any bad decision, and any sin.

People who refuse to forgive themselves give Satan a little piece of their hearts. There is absolutely nothing noble about trying to punish ourselves for our sin. Jesus took our punishment, so everything is paid for. No matter what you have done—even if it's something that happened years ago—I want to encourage you today with these words: The sacrifice of Christ is enough. It's enough to heal you, set you free, restore and redeem your life, and move you toward a greater purpose and destiny than you ever dreamed possible.

My mother-in-law, Miss Kay, is a wise woman. People who only know about her through *Duck Dynasty* may not realize that she is an amazing encourager and that she has a gift for helping people who are struggling through difficult situations. When people talk to her about not being able to forgive themselves, she offers seven simple but powerful words of advice: "Confess it. Own it. And move on." In other words, admit your sin to God and receive His forgiveness, then forgive yourself and get busy living. Life is too short to suffer every day over something God is willing to forgive. So forgive yourself—no matter what you've done—and get on with the good life God has for you!

Chapter 8

STARTING OVER

*If anyone is in Christ, he is a new creation; old things
have passed away; behold, all things have become new.*

—2 CORINTHIANS 5:17

AL AND LISA: We cannot deny that our story includes a lot of
drama. Parts of it read like a bad novel—drunkenness and drugs,
rebellion and lies, complete disregard for our own well-being and
for the people who cared about us. Both of us suffered situations
beyond our control, and both of us made unfortunate, costly decisions. We look back on those days now and can hardly believe the
ways we were thinking and acting. A lot of the things that happened to us were negative and many of the consequences of our
choices were painful, but things were about to take a positive turn.

A NEW LIFE

AL: When Dad baptized me in the Ouachita River, he did so
because I asked him to and he could see a genuine commitment

to Christ in me. He knew I had reached the end of myself after the incident with my girlfriend's husband and that I was serious about making a fresh start with new values and priorities and with Christ as my Savior and Lord.

After having spent my life taking care of my brothers for several years, going through my wild times as a teenager, running from my problems by going to New Orleans, and then having a major wake-up call on the wrong end of a crowbar, I really was ready for a genuine life change—and that's what my faith in God and surrender to His will offered me. I was firmly committed to living a Christian lifestyle, and I knew that no matter how desperately I wanted to live by God's Word, women would be a problem for me because the enemy, Satan, would do his best to bring me down by tempting me with the things I had enjoyed so much in my past.

For the first time since ninth grade, I did not have a girlfriend, and I did not like being alone. But I was determined not to start dating someone just for the sake of dating. I longed for a different type of female companionship than I had known previously, a spiritual union with the right person. Despite my past, after my life-changing encounter with Christ, I had no desire to develop a sexual relationship with anyone outside of marriage. Plus, I still had the "commitment chip" in my emotional wiring, so I soon began to think about the kind of woman I might want to settle down with. I knew in my heart that I was a one-woman man, so I got busy figuring out who that one woman might be. It did not take long. Instead of starting over and trying to meet someone new, I decided to go back to someone I had known for years.

I had not been able to get Lisa off my mind for quite some time, and I felt she still loved me even after all we had been through. I was still a bit arrogant—arrogant enough to think Lisa would probably jump at the chance to get back together with me. Even though I expected her to be eager to reconnect, the way I had treated her previously weighed heavily on my mind; it was the one thing that made me feel flawed in my new life. I wanted to apologize to her,

> I decided to see if the one girl who truly loved me would be willing to start over with me.

but I also wanted to see if my hunch that she still cared about me was right. Even though I'd heard a few rumors about her lifestyle and even learned about the abortion while I was in New Orleans, I soon decided to see if the one girl who truly loved me would be willing to start over with me.

THE CALL THAT CHANGED MY LIFE

LISA: Caller ID had not been invented when Alan dialed my number that day in January 1984, so I was shocked and thrilled— and nervous—when I heard his voice. At that time, during the second semester of my senior year in high school, I was seriously dating the guy with the cool car, and I told Al about him. I also dropped that guy like a hot rock as soon as Alan mentioned the possibility of getting together. The guy was not happy, but the decision to break up with him was easy because I was still in love with Al. This was the moment I'd been waiting for, though I jokingly say now that I knew I would miss the cool car!

I did not care how I had to change my life or what I had to give up. My knight in shining armor was back, and after a wild time of playing the field, he wanted *me*. I could not have been happier. I had not forgotten the pain Al had caused me when he left West Monroe or when I went to visit him in New Orleans. Nor had I forgotten that I had been crazy about him since sixth grade and that he was the only man I had ever wanted to spend my life with.

That first date after Al returned was totally different from any date before. He was committed to treating me well and doing the right thing. He came to my house to pick me up and had to face my parents, who remembered how much he had hurt me and did not know how completely he had changed. Out of their love and concern for me, they were skeptical of him. While they were not rude to him, they gave him a chilly reception when he said hello, and they did not exactly welcome him warmly back into our lives. I understand that, and Al now says, "I corrupted their daughter, took her virginity, abandoned her, broke her heart, then came roaring back into her life claiming to have changed. I totally get why they were not glad to see me!"

A lot of our conversation that night focused on how Al's life had changed. He wanted me to know what a major transformation had happened in him. He felt terrible about the ways he had treated me in the past and offered a sincere apology, which I gladly accepted. He also made clear to me that if we were going to date, our relationship would have to be different than it had been previously. He wanted to do things God's way, which included studying the Bible together, praying together, going to church, and staying sexually pure. All of that seemed like a tall order to me, but I was willing to do anything to please Al and maintain a relationship with him.

On some level, there was also something about the wholesomeness and the goodness of our decision to stay abstinent that I found appealing. The idea of wanting to honor God in a relationship was completely foreign to me, but I agreed to try. I knew Al's parents lived that way, and I had great respect for them, so I thought the whole concept of a godly relationship was worth a try, even though I knew it would be challenging. Besides, Al and I both knew from firsthand experience that nothing good had ever come from being immoral; we had had enough bad things happen to us. The desire to avoid more negative consequences motivated me to stay pure more than anything else.

WE WERE GOING TO DO THINGS DIFFERENTLY

No one who knows much about Phil Robertson would accuse him of mincing words. My father-in-law is a straight-talking man, and he has been that way as long as I have known him. When Al and I got back together, Phil told him, "You've got to cull her or convert her." In other words, he did not want Al to date me if I was not a baptized believer in Jesus Christ.

When Al talked to me about getting baptized, I agreed to do so in order to please him. I could tell that he was on fire for God, and though I did not understand the change in him, I liked its positive results. I had been through enough hardship and heartbreak by that point in my life that I was open to trying to build a growing relationship with Al God's way, even though I had very little understanding of what "God's way" meant.

Because Al felt so strongly about our dating in a God-honoring fashion, we spent very little time alone. We knew that if we did, temptation might get the best of us, and we truly did not want that to happen. To put safeguards around ourselves and our relationship, we hung out a lot at Phil and Miss Kay's house. I went to the Robertsons' home every weekday after school and spent a lot of my time during the weekends there. Being in their home provided the security and accountability we needed to help us stay pure and it gave us a great family atmosphere in which to keep building our relationship.

Al's brothers seemed to like me and appeared to be happy to have me around the house. They were definitely glad to have Al back in their lives. His newfound commitment to Christ was obvious to them, and they were happy to see that he had returned to the stability they were accustomed to in him. But Jase wasn't quite so sure. He had been so angry about what Al had done that Al really had to prove himself to Jase. Jase was skeptical of Al's transformation, but over time, he came to realize that Al's life change was sincere. Willie and Jase were beginning to date at that time, so Al and I got to be involved in that aspect of their lives, which was a blessing to us. Jep was only about five years old at that time, so we took him places or let him tag along on our dates. That was a guaranteed way to make us behave, but we also had a lot of fun with him.

Over the next several months, Al and I talked and talked and talked. He told me all about his time in New Orleans, and I told him about the way I lived while he was away, even though he had heard plenty through the grapevine. I was completely straightforward with him about the mistakes I had made with guys and about the abortion. Both of us shared the difficulties and struggles we had faced, and we dared to dream together about the good life and happy marriage we knew we could have in the future. These conversations brought new levels of depth and substance to our relationship and caused our love to grow in unprecedented ways. Without knowing exactly what we were doing, we developed some good communication patterns and laid a solid foundation for transparency, honesty, and openness, which would prove vital to surviving the relational storms that would hit our marriage years later.

> Both of us shared the struggles we had faced, and we dared to dream together about the good life and happy marriage we knew we could have in the future.

Of course, during that spring of 1984, we had no idea what the future would hold for us. For the moment, we were just happy to be back together. Al had not formally proposed to me, and we had not set a wedding date, but in our hearts we were committed to one another and were confident we would be married within the next year.

SEASONED REFLECTIONS . . .

LISA: When Al and I began thinking about marriage, my parents were still a little nervous about him because of the way he had treated me in the past. Even though he worked hard to gain their favor, they were concerned about my getting back together with him. That meant I did not have a parent to confide in or ask the questions I wanted to ask about the possibility of getting married, even though I was young and not experienced enough to think about my future in the most mature ways. I had not been involved in church very long at that time, so I did not know any older married women who could help me think through what being a wife would mean. All I knew was that I was crazy about Al and eager to marry him as soon as possible.

Now I am a mother myself—and a grandmother. Al and I will write later in the book about our two daughters, Anna and Alex, and their families. Before Alex married her husband, Vinny, she asked me some questions I wish I had been able to ask someone before Al and I married. I want to share part of the letter I wrote her in response, hoping it will encourage other young women in serious relationships that may lead to marriage.

We have to make some mistakes so we learn to be like Christ. How can you learn forgiveness if you never forgive? How do you learn that sacrifice is not really sacrifice if you don't give up your will for someone else? How will you know what it feels like to say, "I am sorry, please forgive me," if you don't make a few mistakes along the way?

I want your mistakes to be as minor as possible, but I know you will make some. I know Vinny will make some too. You can both protect yourselves from the really harmful mistakes by guarding your hearts, your minds, and your marriage. To do this, Christ has to be the center of your life. He has to be the third strand that makes your rope unbreakable.

I love your dad more than I love myself. If there is anything that makes him unhappy, I will die trying to fix it. After God, he is the most important person in my life. But he has to be after God for our marriage to work as God intended it to. Nothing in this life is worth more than your relationship with God and your relationship with your soul mate . . .

Love never fails!

Mom

AL: After Lisa and I got back together, there was one important thing we knew and one we did not know. We knew we were deeply in love and wanted to get married, but we had no idea that God has had a plan for marriage since the very first man and woman set foot on the face of the earth. We loved each other and we loved God, but as we thought about getting married, we were not aware of the importance of making a concerted effort to understand how to transition our relationship from dating to engagement to marriage; nor did we know what we were supposed to do in order to grow emotionally as husband and wife once we said "I do." We did our best to honor God and build our relationship in a godly way, but there was so much we had not learned about how to enter into an intimate relationship. Over the years, we have studied God's plan for an ideal marriage, and we are thankful that we have discovered it. Better late than never!

Now, when we counsel engaged couples or lead marriage retreats, I like to share a simple, four-point summary of God's plan for husbands and wives. This allows me to share with them what we wish someone had shared with Lisa and me as we considered getting married. Whether you are married or hoping to marry or remarry someday, we hope the advice God gave the very first couple will help your existing marriage flourish or your new marriage get off to a great start.

God never intended for men and women to figure out how to be married on their own, so He included a lot of instruction in the Bible. God wants marriages to be great. He wants to bless them, and the key to enjoying a blessed marriage is to live according to what God asks us to do in His Word.

The first foundational Scripture passage we call attention to when we teach about God's plan for marriage is Genesis 2:24–25: "Therefore a man shall leave his father and mother and be joined to his wife, and they shall become one flesh. And they were both naked, the man and his wife, and were not ashamed." These verses are so important that we not only see them in Genesis, which sets the tone for so much of the rest of the Bible, but also in Matthew and Mark. God the Father spoke them first, then Jesus repeated them. That tells us we need to pay attention to them.

In Genesis 2:24–25, we can see God's plan for an ideal marriage—not a ho-hum, so-so marriage, but the best possible marriage. Anyone who is married or thinking about getting married someday needs to understand God's plan for the husband-wife relationship. Without a vision of His ideal, we don't know how great our marriages can be. Once we see what God really wants for us, we can easily recognize where our marriages may fall short, and we can begin to pray and work toward the ideal, knowing that it is possible.

If we look at each phrase of Genesis 2:24–25, we see four keys to an ideal marriage. First, we read, "A man shall leave his father and mother," which tells us that there needs to be a *severing* of past relationships. Second, we see that the man will "be joined to his wife," which means the couple enters into *unity* with one another. Third, "They shall become one flesh," which indicates the *permanence* of their relationship. And fourth, we read, "They were both naked, the man and his wife, and were not ashamed." This tells us they achieve *intimacy*.

Think of these four ideas as pillars that are holding up the foundation of your marriage. If any one of the pillars is not built correctly or is allowed to be damaged or destroyed, it can take down the entire structure, or in this case, the marriage. On the other hand, if all four pillars stay strong, they support a vibrant, healthy marriage.

These four qualities—*severance, unity, permanence,* and *intimacy*—will put a couple in the center of God's plan for an ideal marriage. These things sound good, and they are good, but achieving them takes work and dedication. If anything in life is worth the effort, a great marriage is worth it, so we'll look at the components of an ideal marriage in greater detail in other chapters of the book.

For now, I simply want to encourage couples, no matter where you are in your relationship—seriously dating, engaged, married, or hoping to marry—to take time to understand God's plan for husbands and wives. Marriage in most parts of the world today is under fire, and the only way to build a relationship that will survive and thrive is to do it God's way. Remember that it is *never* too late to rebuild the four pillars the proper way!

> If anything in life is worth the effort, a great marriage is worth it.

Chapter 9

TOGETHER FOREVER

"But from the beginning of the creation, God 'made them male and female.' 'For this reason a man shall leave his father and mother and be joined to his wife, and the two shall become one flesh'; so then they are no longer two, but one flesh. Therefore what God has joined together, let not man separate."

—MARK 10:6–9

LISA: One Friday night after Al and I had been back together in a serious way for about six months, he asked me to marry him. Of course, I said yes, and I was so excited. This was what I had always dreamed of, and I could hardly believe it was actually happening. By then, I had finished high school and was working, and Al was working and going to college. Though we intended to get married the following summer, the summer of 1985, we soon began to realize we did not want to wait that long, so we planned to move the date up to January 1985. Both of our birthdays would be during that month; we would be nineteen and twenty years old. Because we had a strong mutual attraction, we knew "our biology was threatening to overtake our theology," as Al says, and we saw we could not even wait until January. We really did not want to engage in sex before marriage, but like all young couples who are deeply in love and trying to wait for their wedding night, the burden of the struggle to remain pure got to be too much for us. So on November 2, 1984, in the middle of a conversation about something else, Al said, "How about next Friday night?"

I said, "For what? Are you talking about going out on a date?"

He said, "No, for us to get married."

My response was not particularly romantic, but of course, neither was Al's proposal. I did get teary eyed, though, and simply said, "Yeah, I'm in. Let's do it."

That settled it. We had one week to plan a wedding for Friday, November 9, 1984.

Phil and Miss Kay were fully supportive of our getting married, and they had no objection to our doing it quickly. In fact, Phil encouraged Al to move fast once he made up his mind to marry me. But my parents were not excited at all. As much as Al's behavior toward me had changed and as committed as he was to doing the right thing in every aspect of our relationship, he freely admits he did not handle my parents well when we decided to get married. Instead of talking to my father and asking for my hand in marriage, he basically said to me, "I guess you need to tell your parents."

> "Our biology was threatening to overtake our theology," and we saw we could not even wait until January.

Al and Phil when Al was almost one year old in 1965.

Lisa in the first grade in 1971.

Brother and Sister Layton, the preacher and his wife who took a special interest in Al in Junction City, Arkansas, sometime around 1970.

Mr. Pinecrest in 1977! The only title Al has ever had!

Working the leisure suit and the hair parted down the middle when Al was a senior in 1981.

A hot babe in her senior year of 1983–84!

Our wedding pic with Lisa's family on November 9, 1984. On the left are Hoot and Maudie (Lisa's parents), and on the right are Barbara and Bill Wilson (Lisa's sister and brother-in-law).

Our wedding pic with the Robertsons. Miss Kay, Jase, Willie, Jon Gimber (Al's first cousin), and Jep.

Lisa's grandmothers, Ma Gibson (Hoot's mom) and Mamaw Miller (Maudie's mom) around the late 1980s.

Tiny and improving Anna after successful surgery in April 1986.

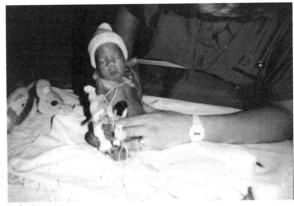

Al and Lisa with Anna and Alex around 1992.

Anna and Alex with Papaw Hoot at Christmas in 1995.

All the Robertsons at Anna and Jay's wedding on July 3, 2004.

Jay and Anna with Anna's two papaws, who gave her away on her wedding day, July 3, 2004.

Lisa and Al at a Valentine's Day Sweetheart Banquet at White's Ferry Road Church around 2004.

Two sisters laying up after Carley Elizabeth Stone, the first grandchild for Al and Lisa, was born, November 27, 2005.

Lisa with her sister, Barbara, and her mom, Maudie, at the White's Ferry Road Church Mother's Day Breakfast in 2008.

Al and Lisa in 2012.

Al and Lisa with Alex and Vinny on their wedding day, which was also Al's birthday, January 5, 2013.

Papaw Phil giving away Alex on January 5, 2013.

The whole crew in 2013 before Sage and Corban were born.

Carley and Bailey Kay playing with "Pap" in the pool in 2012.

The prodigal and the father enjoying a close relationship, working together to impact the world in 2013.

The Duckmen of Louisiana: clockwise from left, Al, Jay Stone, Godwin, Si, Martin, Jep, Jase, Phil, and Willie in spring of 2013.

All four brothers, Jase, Willie, Al, and Jep, sporting beards at the opening of Willie's Duck Diner in October 2013.

August 11, 2014, the birthday of daughter number three for Jay and Anna, Sage Alexis Stone, named after Alex.

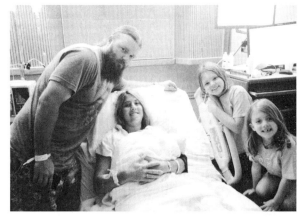

Lisa, with our four precious grandchildren!

Papaw Phil with his first great-grandson, Corban Marshal Mancuso, named after Al, in August 2014.

Al and Miss Kay having fun in front of a large audience in Tulsa, Oklahoma, in March 2014.

The women of Duck Commander (me, Jessica, Miss Kay, Missy, and Korie) getting their shop on in Scotland in August 2014!

Thirty years of love and life! August 2014 in Scotland.

In the months since Al had come back into my life, my mom and dad had seen drastic improvements in my attitude and my behavior. Everything about me had stabilized: I had dropped my bad friends, I went to class instead of skipping school, and best of all, I was happy. They could tell Al was a good influence on me, but they were not ready to embrace him as my husband so quickly after we reconnected.

When they heard we were getting married the next week, they said they would not come to the wedding. I had always enjoyed such a good relationship with my dad that I was crushed that he would not give me away, but I was determined to move ahead with the ceremony.

As Friday drew near, my parents began to change their minds. My mother did contact one of my old boyfriends and ask him to ask me out on a date for the night of the wedding, without telling him my plans. When he called, I told him I was getting married that night! My mom also called the preacher we had asked to marry us and appealed to him to try to convince me to wait and to ask me questions such as, "Don't you think you might regret rushing into this a few years from now?" Or, "Don't you want a nice, big wedding?" No, Al and I told him, we did not.

Those were my mother's last attempts to interfere. I understand now that she and my dad had legitimate concerns about me and they were justified in the many ways they questioned me about my future with Al. At the time, though, I just felt they were trying to keep me from marrying the man I loved. I was sad that they did not support us, but I was not going to let that stop me from going through with getting married. The day before the wedding, my mother bought me a dress I had tried on earlier—knowing I could never afford to buy it. When my parents gave me the dress, I asked them, "Are you coming or not?"

My dad said, "I'll give you away." That, and the fact that my sister, Barbara, agreed to be my maid of honor, pleased me very much.

HUSBAND AND WIFE

AL: Like so much of our lives prior to our getting married, our wedding day had a bit of drama. All of us Robertsons left our place on the river to go to the preacher's house, where the ceremony would be. We had a large white Ford LTD and a small Ford Fiesta at the time. Most of the family climbed in the LTD, since it was the roomier of the two vehicles. There was only one problem with that: The previous day, the LTD was almost out of gas, and Lisa noticed that. She asked my grandfather Pa where to get some gas for it. He told her to get "the red gas can" nearby and put fuel in the car. Lisa poured what she thought was gas into the car, but unfortunately it was kerosene. Pa was either mistaken about the contents of the can, or my family had more than one red gas can and Lisa picked up the wrong one.

A few miles down the road, that big car began to sputter and soon died a death due to kerosene. We left the car on the side of the road and stood beside it in our wedding clothes until the rest of the family drove by in the Fiesta. We ended up piled on top of each other in that tiny car. It was a five-seater at the most, but that day it carried nine people, and we all made it to the preacher's house in time for the wedding.

The preacher's entire family contributed to our big event. He, of course, conducted the ceremony, in their living room in front of the fireplace. His young daughter, maybe ten or eleven years old, played the wedding march on the piano. She tried her very best but hit a lot of wrong notes. Every time she missed a key, one of her parents leaned over and whispered, "It's okay," which hopefully

> Lisa poured what she thought was gas into the car, but unfortunately it was kerosene.

made her feel better. We all thought it was really funny and tried to keep from laughing out loud. After the ceremony, we had a small reception for our guests in the preacher's dining room, with a cake his wife had made.

We certainly did not have a large wedding. The only members of the Robertson family who came were Miss Kay, Willie, Jase, Jep, Granny, Pa, and my cousin Jon Gimber. Phil was traveling and selling duck calls. From Lisa's family, only her parents and Barbara and her husband were able to attend. Both of us had left behind many of our former friends who had been bad influences, so the only one of our friends who was there was the best man, W. E. Phillips, one of my duck-hunting buddies. In addition, about ten people from the church showed up. Not having a crowd did not bother us at all though. We had each other from that moment on for the rest of our lives, and that was all that mattered.

One of the special moments of that day took place when Lisa's dad pulled me aside before the ceremony. He knew I had not handled anything about marrying her in a proper, respectful way, but he also knew I was determined to marry his daughter. He simply said to me, very gently, "Take care of my daughter." I wish now I had initiated that kind of conversation with him and assured him I would be good to her before he came to me. But the fact that he spoke to me that way made a difference in our relationship for the rest of his life. Over the years, he and I developed a good rapport and mutual respect. He could have treated me badly that day, but he did not. I was not mature enough to do the right thing by going to talk to him, but he was mature enough to say the right things to me. I have always appreciated him for reaching out to me with such kindness.

OFF WE GO

One way Lisa's parents expressed their displeasure over our getting married involved the car they had given her—a brand-new 1984 Monte Carlo. We could keep it, they told us, if we made the payments on it. This was our first grown-up moment, because there was no way we could afford the car note, so we had to tell them to keep it, knowing they would sell it. They did allow us to use it for our honeymoon before they sold it, so we left the wedding in a much better transportation situation than when we arrived!

Pa gave us about one hundred dollars for a trip after our wedding. That was *a lot* of money for him and Granny, but they were very generous people, and they wanted us to have a honeymoon. So that cold, rainy night, we headed for Shreveport, about ninety miles from our hometown, for the weekend. The hotel bill and gas took most of our money, so we did not have much left over for any kind of romantic meal together. I specifically remember going to Popeyes' fried chicken restaurant for one of our first meals as husband and wife. It was not elegant, but it was all we could afford, and we were happy.

On our way back from Shreveport, we stopped to pick up our first real car, knowing we would have to return the Monte Carlo to Lisa's parents. My parents helped us purchase a grayish-blue, used Ford LTD from someone who lived between Shreveport and West Monroe. Apparently, the Robertsons were an LTD family! It was not nearly as cool as Lisa's car, but it was the best we could do on our limited income, and it served us well for several years.

Lisa and I did not have money to buy or rent a place to live, so we asked Granny and Pa if we could live with them next to my parents' house.

Lisa and I did not have money to buy or rent a place to live, so before we married, we asked Granny and Pa if we could live in a room in their little house next to my parents. Their home did not have much space, but my big-hearted grandparents welcomed us with open arms.

Granny immediately took Lisa under her wing and began teaching her to cook, and we ate with her and Pa, my parents, and my brothers almost every evening. Lisa had a good job working at a bank, and I hunted ducks every day as part of my work for Duck Commander. In spite of everything we had been through in our dating relationship, when Lisa and I finally ended up together, our marriage felt like it was off to a good, happy start.

SEASONED REFLECTIONS . . .

AL AND LISA: When we married, we did so with the "benefit" of about thirty minutes of premarital counseling at a preacher's house. At least half of that time was spent with the preacher trying to talk us out of our wedding! We look back now and realize thirty minutes of good advice, instead of bad advice, might have helped us get off to a better beginning. In actuality, it would have taken months of solid biblical teaching and counseling to get us off the crash course we were on and put us in position for a great marriage.

One of the biblical principles we mentioned earlier from Genesis 2 is the principle of severance, which is commonly called the principle of "leaving and cleaving." "Leaving and cleaving" means to leave old relationships behind in order to embark on a new one. Severing a relationship with one's father and mother certainly does not mean discontinuing the relationship—extended family relationships can add a wonderful dimension to healthy marriages. But "leaving and cleaving" does mean giving a new relationship with a spouse priority over family-of-origin associations, and it means honoring the husband-wife relationship over the parent-child relationship.

When a man and woman become husband and wife, a new family is birthed. Often, couples don't think of themselves as a family until their first child arrives, but that's not the case at all. A new family comes into being when two people join themselves together in the covenant of marriage. When couples leave and cleave, their marriage becomes a place of sanctuary (where they honor God in the relationship), retreat (from the pressures of life), and safety (from the work of the enemy in its various forms).

One of the things that hurt our marriage was that Al did not sever certain activities with his dad or his brothers after our wedding. Rather than spending his evenings and weekends with Lisa, he often goofed off with the boys and watched late-night television with Phil.

Although financial struggles created the need to live with Granny and Pa next door to Phil and Kay, we now tell couples to try to start with their own space if at all possible. The more independence a couple can gain from their parents and grandparents, the better, but this is a transitional time and it usually doesn't happen overnight.

The idea of severance is emotional and mental as much as it is physical. It's essential that we change our allegiance and shuffle our priorities. Even good relationships with parents, siblings, in-laws, and extended family need to take second place to the marriage relationship.

Healthy severance sets a husband and wife free to be joined to one another. That joining—that coming together of two hearts, two lives, two sets of opinions, two of everything—is what unity is all about. When a couple commits to unity, the focus is not on what they're leaving behind but on the new and wonderful relationship they're entering.

But there's an important distinction between unity and

uniformity. When one spouse tries to be just like the other or lives simply to please the other, that's uniformity, not union. Lisa struggled with this from the very beginning of our relationship; her goal was to please Al. That may seem to work for a while, but ultimately people who conform in this way end up sacrificing who they really are—and become frustrated and resentful.

God created each person on earth with a unique design, and He did this for a reason. When two people come together to be joined in marriage, they bring their unique temperaments and personalities, strengths and weaknesses, likes and dislikes, dreams and disappointments, hopes and fears, habits and feelings. They may also bring different ideas about practical matters such as money management, how to spend holidays, and how to raise children. In an ideal marriage, these differences become assets, not liabilities. Handled properly, differences make teams stronger and keep life interesting.

> Handled properly, differences make teams stronger and keep life interesting.

One key to making these differences work for us and not against us is respect—looking to see what's good about our differences, not what's wrong about them. Another key is deferring to each other's strengths and allowing the other person to take the lead in his or her area of giftedness. In unity, no one gets his or her way all the time. Unity means knowing when one person needs to step up and the other needs to back off. If the same person is always out front, that may indicate domination, manipulation, or control, certainly not unity.

Think about it this way: A university is one institution, but it includes multiple colleges. In the word *university* itself, we can see the ideas of both unity and diversity. No one expects the college of pharmacy to be like the college of art. In fact, the quality of the entire university depends on each college excelling in its specific area of focus. If they are all excellent and work together as parts of a whole, the university is stable and strong.

In joining together a husband and wife, God wants to blend everything about one person with everything about the other, for the sake of strengthening both. The heart of unity is the blending of all these things into a unit that functions successfully in the world, blesses other people, and brings honor to God. The goal is not conformity, where two people are just alike, but unity, where two people are free to be who they are so they can complete each other as they celebrate their differences and mingle them together for the good of the relationship.

Joining together in true unity takes humility, perseverance, and sometimes creativity. But when both spouses are willing to offer themselves completely to the marriage, let go of what may not be helpful about themselves, and embrace what is valuable in each other, great things can happen.

Chapter 10
NEW BLESSINGS, NEW CHALLENGES

"My grace is sufficient for you, for My strength is made perfect in weakness."

—2 CORINTHIANS 12:9

AL AND LISA: The first several months of our marriage were some of the best days of our lives. Sure, we dealt with the same obstacles that many newlywed couples do, and we did not do everything right, but we were still blissfully happy. We did not have much money, so we learned how to live on love. We thoroughly enjoyed living with Granny and Pa, even though the four of us were in close quarters. We often fell asleep at night to the music of Pa's deep bass snore and Granny's light, almost whispering snore. We had the blessing of Robertsons all around us, literally, and when we needed an occasional evening alone, Lisa often fried potatoes for us or made Hamburger Helper or pimiento cheese, and we ate dinner in the little house while the rest of the family ate at Phil and Miss Kay's. Even with our occasional newlywed challenges, the first year of our marriage was a joyful one.

— 121 —

A HOME OF OUR OWN

AL: As much as Lisa and I liked being with Granny and Pa and having all of our family nearby, almost underfoot, we knew we needed our own space. The problem was, we could not afford much. My dad had been trying to buy some property next to his land on the river for years, but the owner, who used it as a fishing camp, would not sell. The property included a little shack, just a combination kitchen and living room and a bedroom—about five or six hundred square feet of living space, plus a front porch and an outhouse.

The people who owned the property visited and stayed in the shack occasionally during the six months Lisa and I lived with Granny and Pa. One weekend, they came to do some fishing and had an unusual experience. The wife was terrified of snakes. When she sat down on a chair and felt something moving under the cushion, she jumped up and ran screaming out of the house. It's a wonder she did not hurt herself. Yes, there was a snake under the seat cushion, and right then and there, the woman announced to her husband that she would *never* set foot in that fishing camp again. Apparently, he knew she was serious, because he soon called my dad to ask if he was still interested in buying the place.

When Lisa and I heard about the situation, we immediately started trying to figure out how we could buy the property and the little shack. By that time, our relationship with Lisa's parents had improved, and they graciously helped us get the place by cosigning for the loan. Granny and Pa chipped in too, even though I am sure that was a sacrifice for them.

This was the mid-1980s, and Lisa and I did not want to live with an outhouse. Lisa's dad enclosed the front porch, and using money Granny and Pa gave us for materials for a bathroom and septic system, Lisa's dad and I put in a small bathroom. We also added a living area. In addition, Lisa's dad built us a kitchen table, and we did as much work as we could on the place during the summer of 1985. We moved Lisa's king-size waterbed, complete with a dome that held a stereo and television and with mirrors on the sides, into our bedroom.

> We may have been living in a shack, but we thought we were sleeping like royalty.

That monstrosity left little room for anything else. We may have been living in a shack, but we thought we were sleeping like royalty. We had our own place, we were still close to our family, Lisa was still working at the bank, and I was working for Duck Commander. Life was good.

A BABY!

LISA: On our first anniversary, in November 1985, I discovered I was pregnant with our first child, due in May 1986. We were so excited! I did not know much about babies but knew Granny and Miss Kay would teach me how to care for a child.

Al mentioned earlier in this chapter that we had typical newlywed challenges. One of those challenges, which we faced from the very beginning of our marriage, was that my bank job meant I needed to live by a certain schedule and structure. I had to get up every morning and be at work at a certain time. When I got home, I had to do whatever needed to be done around the house, and I had to go to bed at a reasonable hour.

Al, on the other hand, had no such boundaries. He worked for Phil, and I'm not even sure I would call their work hours a real schedule. They definitely worked, and worked hard, because they were building what has now become a duck-call empire, but they were not rigid about when they worked or how they got their jobs done. Phil's philosophy was, "If you're hungry, eat. If you're sleepy, take a nap. Just get the job done!" Miss Kay handled the administrative duties, while Phil and Al focused on making and selling duck calls. Al was free to do many of the things he had done before we married, and that didn't bother me much in our early days. But when we found out we were expecting a baby, I wanted him to be home more to help around the house and to pay more attention to me.

Al now says he was a young husband trying to live the single life and that he was responsible for the fact that we violated so many aspects of the biblical concept of severance. He admits he was selfish and did not handle this situation the right way. As a result, I allowed resentment to creep into my heart and thought more than a few times, *He just married me for sex.*

We argued about how he spent his time more than anything else, but not constantly. We had a lot of happy times, punctuated occasionally with tense moments. Growing up in my family, I had seen people argue and yell when they were not happy with each other, so I yelled at Al when I was unhappy with him. I did not know how to have a healthy disagreement or a reasonable conversation, nor did he. We fought and raised our voices more than was necessary and made the mistake of going to bed angry too many times, but overall, we still felt good about our marriage and looked forward to having a happy, healthy baby.

A FRIGHTENING DEVELOPMENT

AL: Lisa's pregnancy progressed normally, and we were excited to start our Lamaze classes in March 1986, about two months before Lisa's due date. On a Friday night, February 28, she began having indigestion and back pain. We didn't know what was going on, so she just tolerated the discomfort, thinking maybe it was related to something she ate or to false labor pains. By Sunday morning, March 2, we knew she was hurting way too badly. Something was wrong, and we needed to go to the hospital.

We arrived at St. Francis Medical Center in Monroe between six and seven A.M. Lisa had only gained about ten pounds, and the nurse who checked us in said to her, "What are you doing here? You don't even look like you're pregnant." She didn't even call the doctor right away.

Before long, they took Lisa to examine her while I sat in a waiting room alone. My parents were at home getting ready for church and waiting to hear from me whether they needed to come to the hospital or not. They did!

About nine A.M. Lisa's doctor found me and asked, "Al, are you ready to have a baby?" I could hardly believe what he had said. A baby? Right then?

There was no stopping the delivery. Lisa had progressed too far, even though she was only twenty-nine weeks pregnant. All those pains she had been having over the weekend were contractions, and we didn't know it.

"There will be complications," the doctor told me. "Neonatal ICU right away," he said. "Fifty-fifty chance of survival." The words echoed through my head. I had never been so frightened in my life.

I was twenty-one years old, all alone in a hospital. In total shock, trying to process everything the doctor had said, I walked to the nearest pay phone to call my parents and Lisa's parents to ask them to come to the hospital.

Before any family had arrived, Elizabeth Anna Robertson was born at 10:10 A.M. that Sunday morning. She was twelve inches long and weighed only about one pound, fifteen ounces at birth. After the intensity of the situation began to calm down, my inner outdoorsman took over and I thought, *I have caught fish bigger than this!*

The doctors and nurses immediately put Anna on a ventilator because she was so tiny. Lisa was in recovery and our parents weren't there, so I walked alone and dazed to the neonatal intensive care unit to see my new daughter.

SEASONED REFLECTIONS . . .

LISA: To say the least, Anna's premature birth was a frightening experience for me as a new mother. With all the uncertainty surrounding whether or not she would live, plus raging postpregnancy hormones, I was a mess. But I also had another problem, which I wrestled with for three and a half years—a problem that could have been solved sooner had I simply understood and embraced the love of God.

One of my biggest emotional struggles after Anna's birth—maybe one of the biggest emotional struggles of my entire life—was wondering if the fact that she came early and had so many problems as a newborn was some kind of punishment for the abortion I had had years previously. People who have never had an abortion may not be able to relate to this feeling, but many women who have undergone that procedure will know *exactly* what I'm talking about. The guilt and shame that come after an abortion, which the clinics don't talk about, can be almost unbearable.

In the "Seasoned Reflections" section of chapter 7, I emphasized the importance of being able to forgive ourselves. Here, I want to focus on the importance of receiving forgiveness from God. These two aspects of forgiveness are both necessary in order to heal from any kind of trauma—whether it's a major loss or disappointment, an addiction or illness, a situation in which we have been victimized, or something else—and move on.

Forgiveness is a thread that is woven through the fabric of most of my life. For almost as long as I can remember, there has been someone or something I needed to forgive, something for which I needed to be forgiven, or someone gracious enough to forgive me. I finally learned that the only way to be free in life is to forgive and let myself be forgiven.

The Bible is clear that being unwilling to forgive is a sin, while willingness to give and receive forgiveness is a blessing. Jesus says in Matthew 6:14–15: "For if you forgive other people when they sin against you, your heavenly Father will also forgive you. But if you do not forgive others their sins, your Father will not forgive your sins" (NIV 2011). Once we ask for God's forgiveness, we can be sure He will give it. In Psalm 51:7–9, David prays to the Lord in repentance for his sin with Bathsheba and says, "Purge me with hyssop, and I shall be clean; wash me, and I shall be whiter than snow. Make me hear joy and gladness, that the bones You have broken may rejoice. Hide Your face from my sins, and blot out all my iniquities."

> I finally learned that the only way to be free in life is to forgive and let myself be forgiven.

As long as I lived in fear that the challenges Anna faced as a newborn were related to my previous sin, I suffered unnecessarily. Once I learned how completely God had forgiven me, I finally reached a place of peace. God has not only forgiven me; He does not even remember my sin anymore. Psalm 103:12 says, "As far as the east is from the west, so far has He removed our transgressions from us," and in Jeremiah 31:34, God Himself says, "I will forgive their iniquity, and their sin I will remember no more." No matter who you are or what you have done, the same can be true for you if you will ask Him to forgive you and then receive the forgiveness He freely offers.

AL: When I teach or preach on marriage, I talk about God's plan for the ideal marriage, which I mentioned earlier in the book, but I also talk about what I call "real marriage." In other words, there comes a time for every couple when reality sets in. Sometimes it does more than just "set in." It hits hard. I'm talking about much more than feeling like the honeymoon is over, though that's usually where reality starts. I am talking about real challenges, real problems, and real pain.

All husbands and wives eventually have to wrestle with the "real," sometimes early in their marriage, as Lisa and I did, and sometimes years later. Sometimes the "real" comes in the form of financial trouble or job loss. Sometimes it's a health crisis in one partner of the marriage or in a family member. It can be any of a number of situations, but when it hits, people know it. Initially, they may feel completely overwhelmed; then they realize they have to dig deeply into their faith and their love for one another in order to first survive and eventually thrive. This is how we felt when Anna was born. We had to decide whether we would allow fear and uncertainty to swallow us or whether we would rise up with the strength God gave us and trust Him—no matter what.

If reality has hit you hard recently and you are afraid,

alone, or confused, let me encourage you to rely on your faith. Trust that God will give you the grace and wisdom you need. Believe that He has good in store for you. Jeremiah 29:11 says: "'For I know the plans I have for you,' declares the Lord, 'plans to prosper you and not to harm you, plans to give you hope and a future'" (NIV). Lisa and I found these words to be true in our situation with Anna, and we have found them to be true in many, many circumstances since then. We believe they are true for you.

Chapter 11

WE NEVER DOUBTED

You will keep him in perfect peace,

Whose mind is stayed on You,

Because he trusts in You.

—ISAIAH 26:3

AL: The medical team was cautiously optimistic about Anna, and they made sure I knew we were in an hour-by-hour situation. They spoke quietly and solemnly, not wanting to discourage me, but they were hesitant to say anything that could be interpreted as particularly hopeful. Everything was "wait and see."

To me, Anna looked like a skinned squirrel. She had little tiny arms and legs, and her skin was so translucent I could see her intestines through it. Her face was narrow and her head was flat; she was almost completely covered with wires, tubes, medical devices, and a central line. She seemed so helpless in her little bed.

I was overwhelmed.

I had tears running down my face as I tried to take it all in, wondering if our baby girl would live and thinking about Lisa and how she would react to this situation. In the middle of our crisis, a nurse walked up beside me and gently put her arm around me. She told me that she too had had a premature baby who was about Anna's size when he was born. Her child had lived, and she encouraged me with their story. She was the first person to ever refer to our daughter as "Anna Banana," a name that stuck for years.

I now realize the nurse's message of encouragement was the kindest thing anyone could have done for me in that vulnerable, frightening moment. Not only was it kind; it was powerful. Something about her words turned the whole situation around for me. As soon as she spoke, I felt a surge of hope and confidence that Anna would be okay. I had no doubt she would survive and eventually be healthy and strong. I had no idea what her journey to health and strength would entail, but I *knew*, somehow, it would turn out well.

FAITH IN THE 40 PERCENT

LISA: By the time Anna was a month old, her condition was worse, not better. Al and I still had not been able to hold her, and we had spent a very somber month visiting her at appointed times in the NICU, where we did not see a lot of victories. We saw some situations that encouraged us and gave us hope, but we saw more that frightened us and broke our hearts. We met some parents who eventually took their babies home to live fairly normal lives and some who left the hospital with empty arms. We felt the weight of Anna's situation and absorbed everything that happened around us, but we also knew God's grace was with us and felt supernatural strength every day.

Nevertheless, we could not deny that Anna was not doing well. She needed to be gaining weight but had lost three ounces instead. She could not be weaned from the ventilator, her color was not good, and her lungs were not developing. The medical team discovered she had a heart murmur and needed surgery.

Through an amazing series of events, the surgeon who would operate on her had once served as the personal physician for the ousted shah of Iran. He was one of the world's very best and had ended up right there in Monroe, Louisiana, after the shah fell. When he told us that a successful surgery would consist of his being able to tie off a duct *the size of a cat's hair* in Anna's heart, we could hardly believe it. It was a delicate procedure, but the surgeon felt confident in his abilities. Things did not look good for her, but we could not shake the feeling that everything would be all right.

The doctors told us Anna had a 60 percent chance of not surviving the surgery. Maybe that's the reason they allowed us to hold her for the first time just before the operation. Now, *that* was an emotional moment! A 40 percent survival rate does not sound very good, but we had complete faith that the 40 percent would win out and she would live. We had no choice. Without surgery, she would have definitely died because her little body sim-

> The doctor told us that a successful surgery would consist of his being able to tie off a duct *the size of a cat's hair* in Anna's heart.

ply had to work too hard to breathe and pump blood. With the surgery, she had a chance.

As concerned parents, of course we were nervous, but at the same time, against the odds, we believed her chances were excellent. We were either too young to truly grasp how frightened we should have been or we had a lot of faith. We now think God simply graced us with a gift of faith for those extremely trying circumstances.

Anna did survive the surgery and soon began to improve. Almost immediately, we could tell by looking at her that her circulation was much better. Slowly but surely, she began to gain weight and become more alert. By the time she was about two and a half months old, she finally came off the ventilator. That was a major milestone for her and for us, because it meant we could hold her. She was eating and drinking from a bottle but still struggled with bradycardia (low heart rate). Sometimes she would forget to breathe, but a good thump on the foot always got her going again. At that time, she weighed more than two pounds—halfway to the four-pound mark, at which we could take her home.

WORKING OUR WAY HOME

LISA: In early June, the doctors gave us good news. Anna was strong enough to be moved from the NICU to a step-down unit called special care. Emotionally, this was good for us because there was so much sadness and there were so many extremely difficult situations in the NICU. We had entered that intense environment every day for about three months and will always be grateful for the wonderful care Anna received there. But for Anna's sake and ours, we were glad to move to a place that meant she was improving significantly. Since the beginning of our journey with her, when Al was filled with supernatural faith that she would be okay, we had never wavered in our trust in God. Still, seeing such an obvious step of progress was extremely encouraging to us.

Visiting hours in the special care unit were less restrictive than in the NICU, so we were able to spend much more time with Anna, holding her and feeding her. Her special care nurse was a good friend from church, Nikki Flowers. Knowing Nikki was taking care of Anna gave us an unusual peace of mind.

As Anna continued to improve, we began talking to doctors and nurses about what to expect once we took her home. They told us she would have to go home with a heart monitor and taught us how to read it. We were nervous about that, but by then we had spent more than three and a half months watching others care for our baby girl and we believed we could handle it. Our friend Nikki helped us know exactly what we needed to do when we got home with Anna—and we are forever thankful to her for that.

When Anna finally reached four pounds, we looked at her narrow little face and tiny body and could hardly believe how much she had grown. Anna seemed so big then, compared to her early days when we had been able to slide a size seven lady's ring all the way up her arm to her shoulder. We were so excited to take her home, and we finally got to do that on a very special Sunday, June 15, 1986—Father's Day.

HOME AT LAST

AL: For about three months after Anna came home to our little house, we could not take her anywhere and could not have visitors. We had to be so careful with her! Thankfully for Lisa and me as parents, we had lots of family nearby and we could interact with them, even though they could not come into our house to see Anna. As much as we believe in the importance of leaving and cleaving, having a family support system right next door to us during those days was extremely helpful.

After Anna's first three months at home, she came off the monitor and people began to visit her. For the rest of that first year, she continued to grow and improve like any normal, healthy little girl. Thanks to God's grace, she had no major health issues.

When Anna was one year old, we took her to the cardiologist for a checkup, hoping and praying all would be well. After all she had been through, we wondered whether she would struggle with heart problems for the rest of her life, but he said her heart was perfect. In addition, her other doctors said she had absolutely no lingering negative effects from her premature birth. She went on to have a perfectly normal childhood and was a calm, compliant teenager. This little girl who got off to such a difficult start is now a beautiful woman, wife to the only guy she's ever really loved, Jay Stone, and the mother of three daughters—Carley, Bailey, and Sage.

SEASONED REFLECTIONS . . .

AL: Anna's health crisis was a huge event in our young marriage. In many ways, people would think it was the worst situation a couple married only about a year and a half could go through, but in the end, one of the worst times of our lives turned out to be one of the best times. It was extremely difficult and extremely rewarding at the same time, especially in terms of our faith and our trust in each other. We clung to one another through that experience. We never fought or argued; we were totally together and completely locked in on Anna. Her situation was a selfishness buster and a faith builder rolled into one.

During that time, we were focused on getting through each day. We could not stop and consider all the things God was doing in our hearts as we walked that agonizing path. Now I see that two specific scriptures became real to us in the midst of our everyday life with a premature infant, passages that might not have been so emblazoned on our hearts without that test of faith. The first was Romans 5:3–4: "We also glory in tribulations, knowing that tribulation produces perseverance; and perseverance, character; and character, hope." The second was Romans 8:38–39: "For I am persuaded that neither death nor life, nor angels nor principalities nor powers, nor things present nor things to

> Anna's situation was a selfishness buster and a faith builder rolled into one.

come, nor height nor depth, nor any other created thing, shall be able to separate us from the love of God which is in Christ Jesus our Lord."

No matter what anyone around us said, whether they were our family or friends or medical personnel, the truths and principles of these verses were at work in my heart.

I could not have said, "I am thinking a lot about Romans 5:3–4 these days," or "In this situation, the verse that I am standing on is Romans 8:38–39," but I know God was putting these truths deep in my heart and in Lisa's as we lived day by day. At that time, we were entirely focused on God and tuned in to Him. We had to be that way, because the medical reports were not always encouraging, and even some of the people who loved us wondered whether we were in denial about the seriousness of Anna's condition.

I think it's fair to say we did not always feel 100 percent supported in our confidence that Anna would be okay. Phil and Miss Kay, in a well-meaning effort to try to prepare us for what could happen, talked to us about how sick Anna was and how difficult overcoming everything stacked against her would be. They were not necessarily doubtful or lacking in faith; they were being lovingly objective and trying to give us a dose of realism that would keep us from a complete emotional meltdown if she did not get better. We knew, though, that they were praying for her to live and that they were fully engaged with us in our battle for her life.

Not only did my parents stand with us during that difficult season, Lisa's parents were also extremely supportive and visited Anna and us often. My relationship with them improved. I really believe our strong faith during those first weeks of Anna's ordeal made a huge impact on both of Lisa's parents, especially her dad.

Lisa's dad developed a special bond with Anna that started in those first days of her life and lasted until his death in 2004. In fact, because I performed Anna's wedding and served as the minister, she asked Lisa's dad and my dad to give her away. What an amazing sight it was for me as a father to see that beautiful young woman—who was not given much of a chance to live when she was born—walking down the aisle as a bride!

During the uncertain and difficult time when Anna's life hung in the balance, we were so thankful to have our parents and families rally around us. In an ideal situation, young parents like Lisa and me would also have been surrounded by ministers who would help build our faith and affirm our trust in God. Our preacher at the time, unfortunately, handled Anna's situation almost the same way he would have dealt with someone clearly at the end of life. He did not encourage us to trust God or pray faith-filled prayers with us.

The way the preacher dealt with us in our greatest time of need was disappointing, but it taught me one of the most valuable lessons I ever learned about being a minister—that a minister's responsibility is to be the person who brings hope and comfort into any set of circumstances, no matter how daunting. People who are under that kind of pressure and are faced with that kind of fear have plenty of others who will tell them how bad things are; we needed someone to tell us how good things could be. I did not realize at the time how often I would be "the minister" in similar settings in the years to come, and how I would use that preacher's attitudes and actions as an example of what not to do. At the time, though, Lisa and I were content and thankful to be in our little house with our happy, healthy baby girl. We consider Anna a miracle, and she and her sister, Alex, have given us some of our greatest joys.

⤙ Chapter 12 ⤛

MORE JOY, MORE PRESSURE

Behold, children are a heritage from the Lord.

—PSALM 127:3

LISA: Any child's first birthday is a big deal, but for us, Anna's first birthday was a major celebration—a *huge* deal, given the fact that we did not know whether she would survive the first week of her life, much less end up a thriving, happy one-year-old a year later. We filled our house with balloons and decorations, and all of our family and friends came to celebrate. We still have a video of all of us happily wearing party hats, eating cake and ice cream. Miss Kay—who would become "Mamaw Kay" to Anna—brought paper dolls, baby dolls, and Barbie dolls. After all those years of raising four roughhousing boys, she was so happy to have a little girl for whom she could buy presents. We thanked God for seeing Anna through such a hard beginning of life and for bringing us through it with so much grace and strength.

About that same time, I found out I was pregnant again. Al and I were so excited to think about giving Anna a little brother or sister. We hoped and prayed for a smooth pregnancy and for my ability to carry this baby full-term and have a normal delivery. Feelings of guilt over the abortion years earlier haunted me again, as they had when I was pregnant with Anna. I still had not forgiven myself, and I spent many days afraid something would go wrong this time.

> Miss Kay—who would become "Mamaw Kay" to Anna—brought paper dolls, baby dolls, and Barbie dolls.

A TIME OF SPIRITUAL GROWTH

Al and I stayed amazed at what God had done in Anna's situation and in our hearts. We talked a lot that summer with each other and with his family about our growing faith. Within a couple of months, most of us Robertsons left the small church we had attended for several years, one fairly close to where we lived. Al and I, and the rest of our family, had been happy there. He led the singing, Phil taught a Bible class, and Pa got to preach occasionally. We were not angry or hurt over anything in the church. Al and I wished the pastor had handled our situation with Anna differently, but we did not decide to leave the church because of that. As a family, we all simply reached a point where we felt the church was not helping our faith grow and realized we wanted a different church experience. In addition, Phil believed we could use our gifts better in a larger environment, and we agreed, so all of us went back to a familiar place, White's Ferry Road. We were so happy to be back at the church that had helped Miss Kay so much when she and the boys first moved to West Monroe and where the whole family had gone after Phil's conversion. Returning to that congregation turned out to be a great decision. We all loved it.

A FALSE ALARM

That summer, I almost went into labor early again, but the doctors were able to stop it. They determined that I had a weak cervix, which is why Anna was premature, and they put in a simple stitch that enabled me to carry this baby to full term. In fact, she was two weeks late! The relief I felt over realizing something fairly minor was wrong with me anatomically was significant. That simple knowledge brought me great peace and was the first step in setting me free from wondering all those years if God was punishing me for the abortion. Once I realized my struggles with pregnancies had an explainable, fixable, physical cause, my longtime emotional and spiritual wrestling with my past began to subside. It did not go away completely, but it no longer struck fear in my heart the way it once had.

Al and I were thrilled with our new baby girl, Katie Alexis Robertson, born November 30, 1987. In those days, ultrasounds were not conclusive and for some reason, we felt certain this baby would be a boy. We planned to name him James Alexander, after my dad (James) and Al's dad (Phil Alexander) and call him Alex. When the baby was a girl, we still liked the name Alex so much that we simply kept it as a nickname for Alexis.

Alex was a happy, healthy baby and an easygoing child. She went through some rebellion in her teenage years, as many teenagers do, and all of us struggled through that season. But she eventually realized the errors of her ways and today she is a trained chef and a wonderful wife and mother. When she married, she wished my dad were there to walk her down the aisle along with Phil. All of us were sad about that and still missed him after his death in 2004. At least she had an escort from one of her two beloved grandfathers.

We also experienced a miscarriage in the fall of 1988. With my having so much trouble carrying our girls to term, we decided not to try to have any more children. We were saddened by the loss as we really wanted a son, but we trusted that God had given us exactly what we needed.

As happy as Al and I were with our two daughters, we also felt the financial strain of a growing family. Even though many of Anna's medical expenses had been written off, we still had significant hospital and doctor bills. With two babies, our household and living expenses also increased, but our income did not. I was the primary breadwinner, and thankfully I had been working at a good job at the bank for a few years by that time and then moved to a better job at a loan company. Al was still trying to help Phil with Duck Commander, which was struggling at that time. Some weeks the company had money to pay him; some weeks it did not.

That year, the number of ducks a person could kill during hunting season was reduced, and that affected Duck Commander's business much more than people might think. A lot of hunters stopped duck hunting altogether because it is an expensive sport and they did not want to invest in equipment if they could not get as many ducks as they had in the past. Others kept hunting but did not buy new accessories, such as our duck calls. Just when we thought Duck Commander was going to survive and grow as a business, the new limits took effect, and the company's customer base shrunk dramatically. The business suffered under the financial pressure of low sales, but Phil still believed in it and so did Al.

> The number of ducks a person could kill during hunting season was reduced, and that affected Duck Commander's business.

Al now says he should not have stayed with Duck Commander full-time during that period without also taking some other kind of job to bring in regular income for our family. He truly had good intentions to help Phil build the business and knew Phil needed his help, but he also realizes now how much pressure that decision put on me. Whenever I spent money, he made comments to try to make me feel guilty about it. I resented that, because I was the one making the money. Besides, I felt he needed to take more responsibility for supporting our family. Money problems, like ours, are so common in marriages and often become the root of all kinds of trouble between husbands and wives. Al and I had no idea how serious the problem was or how far its negative impact would reach into our marriage.

DOING SOMETHING DIFFERENT

While Al and I struggled to make ends meet, we remained thankful that our girls were healthy and growing. We were also happy and extremely active in our church. Several leaders there recognized that Al and Jase, who was only eighteen at the time, had great potential as preachers and influencers, and they encouraged them to attend our church's preaching school. One of the challenges, especially for Al, was that he would have to go to school full-time, meaning we would lose whatever paycheck we did receive from Duck Commander, and he would have to spend time raising money to fund his school fees and to help support our family. I was *not* in favor of that.

After talking about the opportunity to attend preaching school and truly considering it, both Al and Jase responded to the leaders with a polite "Thanks, but we're not interested" answer. But to the family, they basically said, "People who go to preaching school are weird." We laugh about that now, because Al, Jase, and Willie all eventually went to preaching school. Plus, we definitely see the humor in Robertsons calling other people weird!

The following summer, in 1988, the duck-call business had gotten worse, not better. The same gentlemen who approached Al and Jase to talk about preaching school a year earlier came back to try again. This time, they brought a man who could help financially, a man named Alton Howard.

Mr. Howard was Korie Robertson's paternal grandfather—a

smart, personable, successful entrepreneur who spent lots of time, energy, and resources in various ministry endeavors from West Monroe to the far reaches of the world. He promised Al and me eight hundred dollars a month during Al's first year of preaching school. If Al did well, he said he would consider renewing that commitment for the second year. The promise of regular income made preaching school seem more doable for us. Al and I both knew he had a heart and a gift for ministry; we were just nervous about how we would support our family while he trained.

Over the next few weeks, four other couples also related to Korie agreed to support Al with twenty-five dollars a month each, so that gave us another hundred—and we have always been grateful to them for their support. A nearby church offered to support Al as well, so he had commitments for one thousand dollars a month. We soon realized that with my salary too, we would be okay financially if he went to preaching school. So that's what he did, while still helping Phil with Duck Commander, which was barely surviving at that point. Jase also decided to go to preaching school, so the two brothers started classes together in September 1988.

SEASONED REFLECTIONS . . .

LISA: Al saw preaching school and the ministry opportunities that came with it as a new challenge, and he fully
embraced it. He loved learning, and he had always been
smart, so he did well in all his classes. Not long after he
started school, churches began calling him and inviting him
to preach for special occasions, retreats, or youth trips or
to fill in when a preacher had to be away from his pulpit. Al
enjoyed preaching; he quickly became good at it, and congre-
gations liked him and responded well to his messages. From
the looks of the situation, everything was falling into place
for him. He had found his niche and was poised for success as
a minister. Everyone was happy, except me.

I was definitely pleased with the regular financial support
our family received because Al was in school. I also gained
a new level of respect for him as I watched him discipline
himself to get up and go to school on time each day instead
of wandering over to Duck Commander on a loose, unstruc-
tured schedule. In a way, his going to school was a relief to
me because by that time he had spent several years working
for Duck Commander, but the business was barely hanging
on. Several people, and the enemy himself, told me Al would
never be a dependable provider and that he would always
hang around with his parents trying to make the business
work. I was happy to see him set off on a new course, and
I did respect his commitment to school and ministry, but

those were the only things I liked about that season. As Al continued in preaching school, got rave reviews from his preaching assignments, and grew busier with new ministry opportunities, I grew increasingly uncomfortable with the whole situation. All I could think was, *I did not sign up for this.*

For starters, his preaching took him away from home on the weekends, and with two babies, I needed him there. In addition, I did not marry a preacher, and I certainly did not want him practicing his preaching on me! I was happy in our church, but I did not want to listen to ser-mons on other days of the week. I

> I did not have the temperament or the wardrobe to be a minister's spouse.

also did not want to feel I had to do or not do certain things, wear or not wear certain outfits (I admit I liked short skirts, tight tops, and other things that would not have been appro-priate for a preacher's wife, and I did not want to give them up), or hold my tongue when I wanted to say something.

My biggest issue, though, was that I did not want the intense pressure of being a preacher's wife. Every preacher's wife I had ever met had basically the same personality. They were all sweet, gentle, meek, humble, and fairly quiet. None of those adjectives described me. I knew I would never be able to keep my mouth shut if something I did not like were to happen in the church. I just did not have the temperament or the wardrobe to be a minister's spouse. More than those things, though, I had no desire for that kind of leadership role or that kind of visibility in the church.

I now speak often about the fact that being in ministry is like living in a fishbowl. So many people are aware of what takes place in the family of a pastor or minister. This is often extremely difficult for the minister's spouse and children. I did not have any personal experience in ministry when Al decided to go to preaching school. I had simply observed enough over the years to know I did not want to live that kind of life, nor did I want my children to have to endure it.

The more I thought about Al's decision, the more conflict began to boil inside of me. I truly did respect Al for his diligence in school and commitment to his studies, but I also felt such a sense of loss. I had lost him to his studies in the evenings and to his preaching on the weekends—the only times I was off from my job and we could have been together as a couple or a family. Al was totally blind to the way I felt. He was so consumed with school and all that went with it that he did not notice my discontent. I was not at all pleased with the direction our lives seemed to be going in. More than anything else, I missed Al and felt alone. I did not know how to have a healthy, honest conversation with Al about all of this; I just knew I was unhappy. And, after living with growing resentment for about a year, I did not realize I had made our marriage and myself vulnerable to an attack from the enemy.

Chapter 13

DODGING A BULLET

Whoever digs a pit will fall into it,
And he who rolls a stone will have it roll back on him.

—PROVERBS 26:27

LISA: By the summer of 1989, I had left my job at the bank to work for a loan company. When one of my bosses at the bank left to open his own loan company, he asked me to come to work for him—for a nice raise. I agreed. Soon afterward, one of my previous employers ended up in trouble and had to go through a bank investigation. Although I was no longer employed there, I had to answer questions about what was happening in my department while I worked there.

Without going into great detail, I admit I became attracted to one of the investigators. Al and I knew this man and his family, but I never considered him more than an acquaintance until I met with him as part of the investigation and got to know him better. My relationship with Al was strained at the time, and Satan knew exactly how to entice me with a good-looking, stable man who had a good job and who seemed to have his life together.

Anyone who has ever been tempted to build a relationship with someone of the opposite sex outside of marriage may doubt me when I say I did not go into it consciously. But I did not. I had no intention of becoming attracted to that man. Almost before I realized what was really happening, we were involved in a romantic relationship.

The relationship never became sexual, but it almost did. I had booked a hotel room for the two of us, and once I had made those arrangements, the man either got scared or woke up to the impropriety of what we were doing and confessed everything to his wife. She called Al almost immediately, and he was devastated.

STUNNED

AL: By the summer of 1989, I could hardly believe how great my life had become. I had a beautiful wife and two healthy, adorable little girls. My spiritual life was strong, and as I went through preaching school, I felt I was finally pursuing the purpose for which I was created. I was learning so much in school and enjoying great ministry opportunities almost every weekend. Every time I preached, people seemed to appreciate it and responded well to me. I finally realized that the church leaders who encouraged me to attend preaching school were right. I did have potential. I could finally see it and was excited about the future. How lucky could a guy get?

For my situation, a better question is, how clueless could a guy be?

I could not have been more shocked when I answered the phone one afternoon at home after work and heard the distraught but somewhat familiar voice of a woman on the other end. She identified herself as someone Lisa and I knew, not well, but someone with whom we were definitely acquainted.

I listened in disbelief as this woman told me that her husband had just confessed to an inappropriate relationship with Lisa. I did not even know the two of them had been meeting about the bank investigation, much less that they had developed a personal relationship. At first, I refused to believe what the woman told me. But the more she talked, the less I could deny it. I was totally blindsided, but I also realized the woman was telling me the truth. The most painful part of it all was that all the signs pointed to Lisa as the initiator of the relationship.

> I listened in disbelief as this woman told me that her husband had just confessed to an inappropriate relationship with Lisa.

THE NEAR MISS

I went home that day and waited for Lisa. When she arrived after work, I confronted her about the woman's phone call. After talking around the situation for a little while, she eventually admitted it. I literally ran out of the house, shaking and quivering, as though I had been attacked or traumatized in some way. Lisa left for her parents' house.

Immediately, I told my mom and dad what had happened and then went to sit on their boat dock to try to collect my thoughts. One of them must have called a friend of mine from preaching school, because he soon showed up and sat down beside me. He said very little, but he listened at a time when I really needed to talk. I kept saying, "I can't believe it. I just can't believe it." I knew Lisa had not slept with the other man, but what she had done was enough to be truly awful to me.

Lisa stayed with her parents for a couple of days while I stayed in our home with the girls. We did not really separate; we just spent a few days apart. I was hurt, angry, and not sure what to do next; there I was, training to be a preacher, and my wife did not even think I was a good husband.

I continued to speak with the man's wife during this time, trying to figure out what all had happened. Weeks later, I saw the man and he faced me with humility and courage. He was so humbled and so sorry about what he had done. I could tell he genuinely felt terrible about it.

Lisa felt terrible too. She was truly sorry for hurting me. She says that now, in hindsight, she has to admit that her thought was, *I got caught. I'd better not ever do this again.* I was thinking along the same lines and made the mistake of threatening her by saying, "If you ever do anything like this again, I will divorce you!"

In the wake of the infidelity, everything we did for the next several months, we did wrong. We wanted to reconcile, but we really did not know how. We never saw a counselor or anyone else who had the qualifications to help us. Every time we had any kind of argument, I managed to bring up Lisa's extramarital relationship and used it against her.

We never dealt with the core issues, deep feelings, and real challenges that got us to the place where Lisa was so unhappy. Looking back, we say we viewed it as a "near miss" during a stressful time. Even though we did not handle the situation well, we did stay together. The problem was that we did not learn enough from it to let it change us. When I went back to school in the fall, we went back to living the same way we had lived during my first year—the same routine, and unfortunately, all the same relational patterns.

Too Busy to Notice
the Warning Signs

Not long after I finished preaching school, I took a job at our home church, White's Ferry Road. I could not imagine a better place to be a minister than in my own hometown. I did not have to uproot my family. I would be among family and friends who loved me, and I would be in the same church that had provided love and care to my mom and to our family when we first moved to West Monroe with little more than the clothes in our suitcase.

I felt so blessed to have that job. I worked hard and went the extra mile in preparation, serving people, teaching, and leading groups. I even got to travel around the world preaching the gospel. As my ministry stock rose, my marriage stock went down. Lisa felt left out and marginalized, like what we call "second fiddle" in the South. A distance began to grow between us. I could sense something sinister at work against us, but I was too busy or too afraid to dive into it and deal with it. I did what most people do: I ignored the problem.

Lisa and I were busy, like most young parents. We had two growing girls, I had a growing ministry, and Lisa was working for Duck Commander, which had finally started growing too. Lisa certainly had the perfect skills and experience for a job in a small business, but the main reason she went to work there was for safety and accountability. My family had been very disappointed about her relationship with the bank investigator, and my mom thought the Duck Commander office would be a good environment for Lisa. She and Lisa had become very close over the years, and Mom really wanted to protect Lisa from falling into a similar situation a second time.

> I could sense something sinister at work against us, but I was too busy or too afraid to dive into it and deal with it.

Over the next ten years or so, our lives and our marriage rolled along. As I said before, we were busy raising our girls, and we were extremely busy with our church and ministry work. I poured a lot of time and energy into ministry work. I had other pastoral joys and responsibilities too, such as conducting weddings, baptisms, and funerals; making hospital visits; and counseling people who needed help with the struggles of life.

Lisa and I functioned well, and maybe that was our downfall. We kept up with our obligations and we did everything we were supposed to do for our family and our ministry, as best we could at the time. We would later discover that taking care of our family and ministry was not enough. We also needed to be taking care of our marriage. We heard a few alarms and saw a few red flags on occasion, but we did not stop to deal with them. Eventually, our failure to nourish each other as husband and wife and our failure to be proactive in protecting our marriage became a major problem.

SEASONED REFLECTIONS . . .

LISA: After I got involved with the bank investigator, Al and I did everything wrong. We did not call a time-out in our marriage and take time to identify and resolve the problems we faced. Instead, we breathed a sigh of relief that our relationship was not worse than it was. I apologized, and he forgave me because it seemed like the right thing to do, but we were not committed to genuine change. We just kind of moved on.

The problem with moving on was that we were not asking the key question: "Why?"

After several years of working with couples, we now realize that many couples are not willing to look in the mirror and ask the hard questions when there is extreme unhappiness in a relationship. This reminds me of James 1:22–24: "Do not merely listen to the word, and so deceive yourselves. Do what it says. Anyone who listens to the word but does not do what it says is like someone who looks at his face in a mirror and, after looking at himself, goes away and immediately forgets what he looks like" (NIV 2011). We were not really looking and certainly not really doing anything to figure out where our marriage truly was.

The way we dealt with our problems (by choosing not to really deal with them) laid a foundation for a major flaw in our relationship and in my heart. What was that major—and dangerous—flaw? The possibility that I could look to someone other than my husband for what I needed or wanted.

While Al was not aware of what was going on in my situation with the other man, the fact that I got away with that relationship for as long as I did opened my eyes to the idea that I had options. Once that door was open, I had to endure tremendous heartache, fear, and shame before it closed again. Once I agreed with the enemy's lie that I did not have to take my marriage vows seriously, I did not regain the ability or desire to honor them properly for years. Because Al and I never confronted our issues, I never closed my options. I kept them open unconsciously—until the day the enemy tried to take full advantage of them, and I let him.

I often tell people, "If you give Satan an inch, he will sure enough take a mile." We have to realize that we have an enemy, not a little red devil with horns, but a sinister spiritual force determined to steal, kill, and destroy (John 10:10). He plants thoughts in our heads, influences our emotions, and weaves destruction in our relationships. As believers, we know that God wins in the end, because 1 John 3:8 says, "For this purpose the Son of God was manifested, that He might destroy the works of the devil." We can choose every day whether we want to align ourselves with the winning team or whether we will allow the enemy to lead us subtly down a dangerous path. I know what I am talking about. I did this—and I don't want it to happen to you.

> The fact that I got away with that relationship for as long as I did opened my eyes to the idea that I had options.

AL: When I share with couples God's plan for an ideal marriage, which started with Adam and Eve, I can almost read their minds and tell what they are thinking: Of course, Adam and Eve were set up for an ideal marriage! He had a job. He didn't have a mother-in-law. They had a garden full of food to eat and a nice place to live. She did not have a father or a big brother to compare Adam to, and he did not have to stand in line at the grocery store with magazine-cover models making him think his wife wasn't pretty enough! No wonder they had an ideal marriage!

The fact is, Adam and Eve's "ideal" quickly deteriorated into "real" for some of the same reasons marriages become troubled today. All the enemy had to do was tempt Eve to want something more than she already had, and he is still doing that today. Though he started with Eve in the garden, the problem of wanting more is certainly not limited to women. Men are just as guilty, so do not think I am picking on Eve or on women. I am not. Eve just happened to be the one with whom the problem started. I won't go into detail about Adam's role in Eve's sin right now, but I happen to think he contributed to the problem as much or more than she did because he failed to take seriously the leadership role God had given him in their relationship.

Selfishness and greed are two dynamics Lisa and I see at the root of almost every unhappy couple we have ever met. On some level, the reason marriages get into trouble can be traced to one or both spouses wanting more than they have. Someone is dissatisfied and that person eventually starts looking for something to fill the hole in his or her heart. Sometimes, attempts to fill the void seem harmless—a new car, a new outfit, or a nice vacation. But when married people start looking for a new intimate companion, that can ultimately destroy their marriage.

Wanting more is not always negative. For example, it can be good when one spouse wants the other to be more honest or to take more responsibility. But it can be negative, like when one wants to spend more money than the couple has at their disposal or when one wants more freedom instead of growing up and being accountable to the marriage. In Lisa's and my marriage, she wanted a man who was more supportive of her and more available emotionally than I was. I cannot blame her for that; I admit my studies and ministry opportunities did distract me from my marriage and family. I deeply regret that now, and I have apologized to Lisa for it. Thankfully, she has forgiven me as I have forgiven her for looking outside our marriage to find what she felt was missing. My problem was that I just chose to ignore the way she felt—and that was a huge mistake.

Whether you are a man or a woman, a husband or a wife, if you feel even the slightest interest in looking for "more," let me urge you to resist the temptation. Have an honest conversation with your spouse, make your needs and desires known, and do your best to work together to reach the level of fulfillment God intends for you to enjoy in marriage.

Chapter 14

REAL TROUBLE

When the enemy comes in like a flood,
The Spirit of the Lord will lift up a
standard against him.

—ISAIAH 59:19

LISA: My job at Duck Commander was to take and ship orders. One day in 1998, I was going about my business as usual when the phone rang. An old boyfriend from my wild days in high school had contacted us to order some of our duck calls. The only time I had interacted with him since high school had been several years earlier, when I realized that this man and his family lived down the street from a house Al and I had recently rented.

I had no idea these people were our neighbors until the man brought Alex to our door one day. Not knowing she was my daughter or that Al and I lived on his street, he had seen her in a scary situation with a dog and stepped in to protect her. That interaction was very brief. We simply said hello and exchanged "Good to see you"s. Then I thanked him for making sure Alex was okay, and he left. That was the first time I had seen him since high school, and I did not see him or hear from him again until 1998, when I heard his voice on the telephone.

When he called Duck Commander that day, we started out talking business. Once he placed his duck-call order, we moved on to small talk. When I asked about his family, he told me he was separated from his wife. As the phone call concluded, I asked if he wanted me to mail the duck calls.

"You could just deliver them," he answered. I was surprised and intrigued by that response. In the span of just a few minutes on one phone call, Satan planted a seed of darkness in my heart.

> It seemed like an innocent delivery, but it was the beginning of a full-blown fourteen-month affair that almost cost me everything.

I did not know it at the time, but that darkness would grow to the point where it would eventually overtake me.

I made the mistake of taking the duck calls to him at home. After all, I knew where he lived, and it seemed like an innocent delivery. It was not; it was the beginning of a full-blown fourteen-month affair that almost cost me everything.

I tell people now: if you have ever had an intimate relationship with someone and are now married to someone else, don't even allow a casual reconnection. It's just safer that way. Getting reinvolved with someone from your past may seem harmless but can quickly spin out of control. It's like trying to learn to juggle with a live grenade. It gives the evil one an open door to destroy you, your spouse, your marriage, your children, your extended family, and your friends. The reason for this is that while you may have the most innocent and honorable intention to "be friends," you never know someone else's intentions. In my situation, this man's wife had run off with his best friend. He felt betrayed, so he was willing to betray someone else, namely Al.

I KNEW IT WAS WRONG

So many times in my life, going back to my teenage days, I knew something to be true but found myself unable to admit it. This affair was no different. I knew what I was doing was so terribly wrong and so many times I wanted to come clean and tell the truth. But old words reverberated through my mind: *"If you ever do anything like this again, I will divorce you!"*

I was afraid Al would leave me forever if he found out. So I devised increasingly complicated plans to spend time alone with this man and spun increasingly deceitful stories about why I was not at home as much as I used to be. I lived a double life, and it was absolutely horrible.

I was so inescapably miserable that I often thought, *I don't want to kill myself, but if I could just run my car into a tree or drive off a bridge "accidentally," this would all be over.* I hated myself, yet I felt trapped and powerless to stop my wrong behavior.

In the midst of my sin, I remember praying, "God, please open some kind of door to help me get out of this." But when God did open a door, such as giving me an opportunity to confess to a trusted friend, I thought, *Oh no, God, don't make me tell her!*

So I kept my secret to myself, stayed miserable, and kept finding ways to hide the reality of my life.

I never stopped loving Al, even though I was intimately involved with another man. That may be almost impossible for some people to believe, but for others—well, others will understand completely. Something in me drove me to feed the darkness inside me; it kept me keeping secrets and spinning webs of deceit, especially where Al was concerned. He was the one person in the whole world I truly did not want to hurt, yet I kept hurting him behind his back, day after day.

SOMETHING WASN'T RIGHT

AL: During the summer of 1999, which I now know was about three-fourths of the way through the affair, a major fight erupted between Lisa and me because I felt she might be seeing someone. I could not put my finger on exactly what I thought was going on or even articulate my feelings clearly; I just knew something was wrong. Eventually, I grew suspicious enough to confront Lisa about it. She lied and denied everything. Some of our close friends were aware of our tension, and Lisa lied to them too—to the point of influencing them to believe I was simply being judgmental, overprotective, controlling, and ridiculous. They began to look down on me for not trusting her, and I began to think I was crazy.

Though Lisa did not admit to the affair at that point, we both agreed that our marriage was in trouble. We publicly shared with our church that we were struggling and needed their prayers, and we started seeing a counselor. Nothing really changed, though, first of all, because Lisa was not willing to tell the truth in our counseling sessions, and second, because we wanted a fairly quick "fix." We wanted to feel better in our marriage, but we were not ready to do the hard work of dealing with our issues.

Lisa says now that the counseling helped her feel a little better because she thought if we were working on our marriage, she might find the strength to leave her other relationship. But because she would not tell the truth, she did not find much strength at all—just enough to continue living the lie. Our weeks in counseling provided a little relief from the stress we were living under, but I believed something in the dynamics of our relationship was still shifting in a serious, negative way. Something between us was terribly wrong, and I knew it. I could feel it in the pit of my soul.

In addition to my strong belief that something was not right, I noticed that Lisa was gone from home more and more. Sometimes her inexplicable absences lasted just an hour or so, sometimes longer. When I questioned her about where she was going, I felt certain she was lying to me. I felt I was walking on eggshells around her all the time, and I had an inner sensation that a battle was about to break out. Everything seemed to be caving in on me, though I didn't know why.

About that time, Lisa and I went on a cruise we had had planned for months. It was not fun. Lisa now says one of the reasons she wanted to go on that trip was that she knew it would allow her to spend a whole week not having to juggle her two lives. She truly hoped her time with me, away from the other man, would give her the strength and courage to break off her relationship with him. It did not.

When we returned home, I was so conflicted and so confused I felt like I was losing my mind—and I knew I was definitely losing my marriage. While I was trying to provide excellent teaching and spiritual leadership in a large church, the pressure on both Lisa and me was as high as it could possibly have been. Something had to give, and I cried out to God for revelation and relief.

I finally got the revelation, and it broke my heart. I came across hard evidence of the affair, in the form of cell phone records. Once I saw them, I knew. I knew an inappropriate relationship was going on, I knew how long Lisa had been involved in it, and I knew how often Lisa was talking to this man. I was able to basically map the relationship using phone records. I was furious and devastated.

I did not confront Lisa immediately. I spent a good bit of time in discovery mode, getting my facts together, before I finally spoke to her about it one Friday night. She knew early in the evening that I was upset. We went to a football game that night, and I was beyond silent. I was seething, hardly saying a word. She knew something was about to blow up. I felt completely shredded inside, mostly because I wanted the truth so desperately and did not think she would tell it.

When I first confronted Lisa, about nine or ten o'clock that night, after the girls were in bed, she denied the affair. Then she tried to make it seem much more casual than it was, saying, "Nothing ever happened." I knew that was not true, so I kept pressing her. I was aggressive and focused in my questioning, determined to get the truth out in the open, no matter how ugly or painful it might be.

After working through quite a few layers of dishonesty and denial, at about three o'clock that Saturday morning, Lisa finally broke and admitted the affair. When I pressed her for details, she said, "If I tell you everything, you won't love me anymore."

She was so afraid I would leave her, and she did not want our relationship to be over. But she had also believed me when I told her previously that I would divorce her if she ever got involved with another man. I'll never know how much easier admitting the affair would have been for her, or how much sooner she might have done it, had her fear of my divorcing her not been so controlling.

At that moment, when all of this was coming to light, I did not know whether I would eventually divorce her or not. I did know I would not just dump her right then and there. I tried to convince her I would not walk out on her but that I needed answers. She finally said, "Yes, we've been sleeping together for over a year."

Strangely, I felt a calm, peaceful sense of relief, while Lisa completely fell apart, sobbing almost uncontrollably.

I continued my interrogation until about five o'clock in the morning. Then I called Lisa's best friend, Paula Godwin, who is also the wife of my best friend, John, better known today as "Godwin" on *Duck Dynasty*. All I could say, basically, was, "I don't know what's going to happen, but I don't want Lisa around me or the girls. I'm not sure what to do next, but she is going to need you in her life to help her through this. Can you come over?"

The first thing Paula said to me was, "I am so sorry." She was certainly sorry about the affair and the pain it was causing me, but she meant more than that. She was so sorry she had believed Lisa all the times Lisa accused me of being oversensitive and judgmental, even crazy. Paula recognized immediately that my suspicions had been right all along and was sorry for believing Lisa's lies about me.

> "The girls are staying here. You're leaving," I told Lisa. "Now go pack your stuff and get out."

Within minutes after we hung up the phone, Paula arrived at our house. With her standing there listening, the first action I took in response to Lisa's affair was to ask her to leave our home. "The girls are staying here. You're leaving," I told Lisa. "Now go pack your stuff and get out." A little while later, Lisa climbed into Paula's car, and the two of them drove away. I had no idea what would happen next.

Standing there after Lisa left, with the girls still asleep in the house, I had never hurt so badly in my life, and I remember thinking, *Now I understand what I did to Lisa years ago.* I also imagined for one second what God must feel like when his children hurt and betray Him. But I could not dwell on that. I had to take care of our daughters and find a way to lead our family through this nightmare, starting that Saturday morning.

SEASONED REFLECTIONS . . .

LISA: When Al and I look back on this time today, we realize that what drove me to cheat on him had its root in my childhood abuse. This is no excuse for my behavior; it's simply a statement of what I believe the root cause of my problems to have been. As we have spoken with other couples whose marriages have suffered an affair, we have learned that a sinister bond exists between abuse and infidelity. We cannot explain this psychologically, but we have observed it to be true experientially.

I am convinced the first and most dangerous seed of darkness ever planted in my life took root when I was sexually molested as a child. Not only did his inappropriate behavior violate something deep and sacred in me, it was also the reason I learned to hide my true feelings and to keep secrets. That was the time in my life when I began to believe my sole purpose for living was to please men and to be what they needed me to be. It was all so sick, so wrong, and so far-reaching.

Childhood sexual abuse of any kind has severe ramifications. The biggest problem with this is that victims often feel so ashamed or so dirty or so "wrong" that they never process what happened or tell anyone about it. So they go through life making one mistake after another (some of them tragic)—and they become masters at keeping secrets.

Secrets are nothing more than hidden dishonesty, kind

of like what happens when a person talks about a situation but does not tell the whole story and leaves out important points that would make a big difference. Secrets rob you of lasting relationships. They are ticking time bombs that Satan sits on until he sees an opportune time to expose them—the worst possible time for you and the best (most devastating, destructive) time for him.

When a relationship is built on secrets, it's just a matter of time before it all blows up in your face. If you have secrets or hidden sins that you think are buried and will never surface, you are wrong. You are walking on top of hidden land mines. One misstep, one slip of the tongue, one lie that doesn't add up—and it's all over.

If you hold secrets in your heart, hoping no one will ever find out about them, let me encourage you to take that power out of Satan's hands and give it to God. Trust Him to take it and eventually use it for your good. One way God has used my experience with secrets for good is that because I know how destructive secrets can be, I teach my granddaughters that there are no secrets between them and me. They know they can tell me anything and we will work it out. These girls will not grow up as I did; they will grow up knowing the truth will set them free (see John 8:32).

In his book, *The People Factor*, Van Moody summarizes the damage secrets can do to individuals and to relationships:

Most of us are familiar with the saying, "What you don't know won't hurt you." The problem with that assertion is *that it's wrong. What we don't know can hurt us; in fact, it can destroy us and devastate our relationships. Secrets build invisible walls around us, walls that other people perceive but cannot penetrate. What we don't know [secrets] also prevents transparency, openness, and intimacy. It forces us to tiptoe around certain subjects, and it will keep us from giving all of ourselves to another person and from fully receiving all the good others offer us. Keeping secrets will exhaust us, perhaps frighten us, and ultimately separate us from the people we love.**

I couldn't agree more! My secrets definitely separated me from the people I loved and came within a razor-thin margin of devastating the relationships that meant the most to me. I now also know the powerful and transforming truth of Romans 8:28, that "all things work together for good to those who love God, to those who are the called according to His purpose." Everything about my secrets was bad, but God has ultimately used it all for good. Not only am I teaching my granddaughters not to keep secrets, God is also allowing me to expose the harm secrets can do and help lead other secret-keepers out of darkness into honesty and truth.

Don't let another day go by with the time bomb of secrets attached to your life. I quoted this statement from Miss Kay earlier in the book, but it's worth repeating again. Regarding

---

* Van Moody, *The People Factor* (Nashville, TN: Thomas Nelson Publishers, 2014), 117.

the sin in our lives, she says: "Confess it. Own it. And move on."

AL: From the vantage point of the "victim" in Lisa's affair, it would be easy for me to say everything was her fault and that I just married a bad person who proved that she couldn't be faithful to me. That was my early instinct when the truth finally came out. It was also the advice of a lot of friends and family who meant well and were trying to help me. But over a little time, I learned that this oversimplified way of thinking was not true.

> My betrayal of Lisa as a young man, my threats, my willingness to be the lord of her life— all contributed to the recipe of a brewing disaster.

I make no excuses for Lisa's behavior. What she did was terribly wrong and would have been enough to wreck most marriages permanently. In my case, when some of the pain had subsided, I was able to look at the totality of our relationship and see how I had contributed to the setup of this disaster.

Affairs aren't usually built in a bubble; they are crafted by the evil one over a period of time. Like earthquakes, they build slowly with time and pressure until one day they release and explode with devastating results. My betrayal of Lisa as a young man, my threats, my ignoring of problems in our relationship, my willingness to be the lord of her life—all of these issues contributed to the process and the recipe of a brewing disaster. Satan was the mastermind of the affair, and Lisa was a willing participant, but there were other contributors as well—the abuse she suffered as a child, other illicit relationships, our problems, and the man with whom she conducted the affair.

I have since learned that a healthy, honest relationship with God and an honest, working marriage are the best defenses against affairs. Lisa and I no longer keep secrets in our marriage, and the results of that one decision, in addition to other healthy choices we have made, have been amazing.

Chapter 15

HITTING BOTTOM, LOOKING UP

In my distress I called upon the Lord,

And cried out to my God;

He heard my voice from His temple,

And my cry came before Him, even to His ears.

—**PSALM 18:6**

LISA: Early Saturday morning before I left home, I went into our backyard, put my face on the ground, and said in total desperation, "God, I can't get any lower. I have to find some kind of relationship with You." Even though I had gone to church for years, had attended Bible studies, had hosted gatherings of believers in my home, and was a minister's wife, I was not really a Christian. I had never surrendered my life to Christ in a sincere, personal way. That morning was the first time I truly sought God. I knew He was the only one who could help me, and I was determined to do whatever it took to build a genuine relationship with Him.

Over the next several days, I thought a lot about my relationship with Al and about why I felt I had to be baptized in order to date him. After the first date we had when he got back from New

Orleans, I clearly understood that I was expected to become a Christian if I wanted to be involved with him. In order to gain his approval and the approval of his family, I was baptized. Unfortunately, I did not take Christ into consideration when I made that decision.

Baptism should be an outward expression of an inner surrender to Him and should represent a person's decision to relate to Him as Lord. I did not do that. Even after I was baptized, I related to Al as my "lord," meaning I was so in love with him that I worshipped him, as I mentioned earlier. I have heard people jokingly say they "worship" a boyfriend or girlfriend because the infatuation is so great, but I don't think it's funny. I know firsthand how much damage out-of-control adoration can do to a relationship. I made that mistake with Al, and it came back to haunt us in the worst kind of way. I was now living with its unbelievable, painful consequences. When I was baptized as a teenager, I did not understand these things. All I knew was that I was madly in love with the man of my dreams. Now, years later, because I had been living a lie, I had devastated that dream man and turned our lives into a nightmare.

I had been around enough Christians at that point to realize that my only hope—the only way to save my marriage and to be saved from myself—was for me to get serious about God. I had also been in church long enough to know what I needed to do, so I did not waste any time doing it. In my heart, that Saturday night after Al asked me to leave our home, I made a sincere commitment to Christ for the very first time.

COMING CLEAN

Paula took me to stay with a longtime friend of ours from church, a single woman named Laura who had a nice extra bedroom in her home. When I went to sleep that night, my heart ached for my family, but I understood why Al asked me to leave. I tossed and turned as I thought about what the next day would bring—the need to face my family and friends at church.

Going to church that next morning was grueling. I truly felt like the woman caught in adultery in the story Jesus tells in John 8:3–11. Walking through the crowd that day, I was deeply ashamed. Some people were so hurt by my actions and so angry with me that I could feel it. I could tell that some people made an effort to avoid me, while others looked at me sympathetically and then glanced at the floor because they did not know what to say. Still others expressed compassion, and I will always be grateful to them. Putting myself among the people at church that morning was a brutal experience, but I had to do it. That "walk of shame" was the beginning of my journey to healing and wholeness.

The church service was typical—everything I was accustomed to on a Sunday morning, except Al. He normally provided leadership to the service in some way or another, and his absence was especially noticeable that day. Toward the end of the service,

> Going to church that morning was a brutal experience, but I had to do it. That "walk of shame" was the beginning of my journey to healing and wholeness.

our church allows an opportunity for people to walk to the front of the sanctuary for various reasons, such as wanting to share a prayer request with the congregation. I had a prayer request all right, and it was going to be a bombshell.

One of the church leaders stood before the congregation that day as I sat in the front row surrounded by people who loved me and wanted to help me. He read a letter I had written to the church the night before. In the letter, I was completely broken, as straightforward and truthful as I could be, acknowledging exactly what I had done—and admitting that I had been a Christian imposter for years. I confessed that I had tried my best to play the part but never had a genuine relationship with Christ. I did not try to hide or gloss over anything; I laid it all out there, and people were devastated. Many of them viewed Al and me almost as family; that's how close they felt to us. And, of course, our Robertson family was there. None of them knew I planned to address this matter publicly that day. They were not surprised by what I said, but the fact that I admitted my sin to such a large group was as big a shock to them as to anyone else.

That morning was the beginning of my turnaround. No doubt, God had been working on me for quite a while. Otherwise I would not have been so ready to confess my sin, repent, and commit to a new way of life. First John 1:9 says, "If we confess our sins, He is faithful and just to forgive us our sins and to cleanse us from all unrighteousness." For as long as I could remember, I had been entrapped in secrets. That day, when I publicly confessed and the secret came to light and I took responsibility for telling it, freedom and restoration finally became possible.

My Turn Down Front

AL: The Sunday after Lisa went down front to have her letter of repentance read, I stood before my church family at the end of the service to make a statement. Gone was the confident spokesman; gone was the "together" preacher. I was still reeling from Lisa's revelation, and I was still mad. And so hurt. As I turned to face this group of people who had loved me since I was a teenager, I saw that all eyes were fixed on me. Sober, expectant faces waited to hear what I had to say. I don't remember my exact words, but the gist of what I said was that I didn't know what the future would hold. I didn't know if I could forgive Lisa, and I didn't know if we would be reconciled. I had no words of hope for myself or anyone else. That morning, the thought of forgiveness and a restored marriage seemed distant and out of reach. I didn't even know if I wanted to reach for it. Lisa had experienced a turning point in her faith, and she felt hopeful. I did not share her feelings—not yet.

Little by Little

LISA: The week I went forward at church, I began attending Bible study groups and support groups at Paula's house and reading the Bible daily, especially Psalms and Proverbs. I could relate to the brokenness, heartache, and hope I saw throughout the psalms, and I was desperate for the wisdom I found in Proverbs. Little by little, day by day, the words of Scripture transformed the way I saw myself, the way I thought about God, the way I viewed my life, and the way I wanted to live. Soon afterward, I also started counseling, and this time, I was serious about facing my issues and getting help.

The people at our church were amazing. Al and I look back now on those difficult days and realize that we were so well loved. Some people were angry with me for hurting Al, and some chose to be judgmental, but a lot of people demonstrated the kindness, compassion, and mercy of Christ toward me. That does not mean they approved of what I did. It means they were aware of it and disappointed by it, but they were also willing to pray for me, support me, and try to love me into a place of healing, restoration, and strength.

THERE'S MORE

One reason I had time to invest in Bible study and church groups is that I ended up without a job almost immediately after I admitted the affair to Al. Phil and Miss Kay felt that in light of the uncertainty and turmoil in my relationship with Al, the best course of action for the family and for Duck Commander was to fire me.

About a week later, Miss Kay told Al about another mess I had created at work. Duck Commander had already let me go, so they could not fire me again, but what I did would certainly have been grounds for terminating my job.

Miss Kay oversaw the administrative and financial aspects of the business for years. One day, someone from a credit card company called her and asked her why Duck Commander had so much activity in terms of credit activity on our account. Miss Kay knew nothing about it but soon found out I had been crediting my personal credit card from the business account. In other words, I was embezzling money. It was the only way I knew to fund the affair—buying him gifts, buying myself new clothes and expensive makeup. I tell people now, "When you double your life, you double your expenses." That relationship was costly in every possible way.

I could hardly believe the way my world had crashed down on me. In just a couple of days, I had basically lost my husband, my home, and my job. When I say only God could help me, I mean it. Many people would think I was beyond redemption—and some did think so at the time. But God saw me differently, and thankfully so did Al.

What to Do

AL: In the wake of the devastation I felt after Lisa admitted to the affair, I simply wanted to get away from home for a few days. My aunt, my mom's sister, lived in Houston, Texas, so Mom, the girls, and I went down there for a visit. My aunt Ann has always been very close to my brothers and me. When we were growing up, we spent a couple of weeks every summer with her and her husband, Uncle Wade. She and her family were always members of a country club, and we really enjoyed swimming in the pool there. Uncle Wade is the one who taught my brothers and me to play golf, a sport that is still one of our very favorites. Now Aunt Ann goes with us every summer on our Robertson family vacation.

When anyone faces a ferocious mental, spiritual, emotional, or relational battle, it's amazing how much we need to return to a safe zone and hide for a little while. Aunt Ann's house was a safe zone for me, and that was what I desperately needed as I faced a ferocious battle for my marriage. My time with Mom, Aunt Ann, and the girls was exactly what I needed. It enabled me to escape the turmoil in West Monroe and allowed me some time to deal with the immediate impact of what had happened with Lisa.

> **When we face a ferocious mental, spiritual, emotional, or relational battle, we need to return to a safe zone and hide for a little while.**

When we returned, after about a week, I felt stronger and I knew I could face people and deal with the questions, pressures, and decisions I needed to make.

I had to admit Lisa had done everything I asked her to do after the revelation of her affair. She had also been extremely brave and amazingly humble when she publicly took responsibility for her sinful choices and admitted her need for help. I could tell she was sincere about changing her behavior, but

I was not ready to "forgive and forget" and allow her back into our home. Everything from divorce to trial separation to the possibility of reconciliation had crossed my mind.

My family is a close-knit bunch, and they were all aware of what Lisa and I were going through almost as soon as I was. Some of them told me to leave her, reminding me of the near miss several years earlier and saying I was blind to her obvious faults. They thought she would never change, and they urged me to cut my losses and move on. They were very hurt over the whole situation and thought I just needed to be practical and let Lisa go. My mom, however, was more neutral. I think she still saw something redeemable in Lisa—and so did I. I fully understood the seriousness of Lisa's actions, but in spite of them, something in me was not ready to give up on her or on our marriage.

Over the next several weeks, Lisa stayed involved with our daughters, who were about twelve and ten years old, hoping to keep their lives as normal as possible under the most abnormal circumstances. I saw how much they needed her, so I had no problem with her being in our home to take care of them and do "mom things." I was not mean or disrespectful to her, but I did keep my distance. I never touched her and did not talk to her unless some communication was absolutely necessary.

Both Lisa and I could see that having her close to the girls was positive for them and for her. It was hard on me, but I knew how confused and upset the girls were over everything that had happened, and I wanted the best for them, even if Lisa's presence made me uneasy at times. When I found out that John and Paula had agreed to let her live with them for a while, I thought it was a good idea, so she soon moved from Laura's house into a room at their house. They lived across the road from us, which made Lisa's going back and forth much easier and gave her better access to the girls. I think her being nearby and with such close friends was also helpful and comforting to the girls—and they needed all the comfort they could get.

SEASONED REFLECTIONS . . .

LISA: When I speak publicly about my journey, I often share a message entitled "The Men of My Life." After I finally admitted the affair to Al, I had to do a lot of thinking about all that had happened to me over the course of my life and all I had done to hurt myself and other people. As I pondered those things, I saw a connection between the men who have influenced my life and the decisions I made. Let me share a portion of that message, and you'll see what I mean.

The first influential man in my life was my dad. I loved my daddy and he loved me. I only have good memories of my dad, although together we went through a lot of heartache. In my teenage years, I caused most of that pain, but I caused even more later in life when I failed my family extensively. My dad was my hero, my friend, and my cheerleader. Unfortunately, he was also my first god.

The next man to influence my life was my brother. As a child, I was so proud of him for his service to our country as a marine. In fact, I learned the marine theme song and sang it enthusiastically for him when he graduated boot camp. My brother had many hurts, habits, and hang-ups. To medicate the pain of those things, he drank and eventually died of alcohol-related illness at the age of fifty-seven. In spite of his struggles, he was always a hero to me.

The next man who influenced me was not honorable, and he represents nothing but lies to me. I do not need to say much about the man who molested me because I have already written about the fact that he did detestable things to me from the time I was seven years old until I was a teenager. The reason I refer to him as "influential" is that his actions so damaged my self-image, my sense of self-worth, and my idea of relationships. As a result of his interaction with me, I developed a flawed understanding of my purpose in life. I came to believe I existed to satisfy men. That was not true, but I believed it, and that belief ultimately caused much pain in my life and in the lives of people around me.

The most influential man on earth to me is one I met when I was in the sixth grade. It was Al, and you know a lot of our story by now.

During the time Al and I were not together when I was in high school, I dated several other men and even became pregnant by one of them and had an abortion, as I mentioned earlier. I now realize that many of the men in my life gave me nothing positive. With every hurt or violation associated with them, a piece of my soul withered and died.

> With every hurt or violation associated with the men in my life, a piece of my soul withered and died.

Once Al came back into my life, I had no idea how to relate to him in a healthy way. I not only thought he was God's gift to me, I basically treated him as though he were my god. When we married, I saw myself first and foremost as the "wife of Al," not as the bride of Christ. That caused all kinds of problems.

The next influential man in my life was the one with whom I had the affair. His influence was 100 percent negative. Maybe the only redemptive thing about that relationship is that God used it to bring me to the point of absolute brokenness and devastation, a place where I had to either live or die emotionally, a critical, life-changing moment where I would either reach out to Him or continue to spiral downward.

Once I admitted the affair, I felt such relief. No more secrets, no more hiding, no more feeling worthless. Sometimes I remember lying in our backyard with my face to the ground crying out for God to save me like it happened yesterday. I remember the sincerity and desperation with which I cried, "If I am worth anything to You, Lord, please save me." I still get chills when I recall the way God answered me, with an undeniable impression that said: "You are worth everything to Me. I gave My only Son just for you. Had you been the only person on earth, I would have done that just for you." I was undone.

That leads me to the most influential man I have ever known. During the time Al and I were apart, and after the long string of men who went in and out of my life over the years, I finally allowed the greatest, most important man in my life, Jesus Christ—the One who changed everything for me—to rule my life from that moment until eternity. In the wake of having to leave my home and family, I studied God's Word intensely. I prayed. I asked God to be the one true God who would save me, would never leave or forsake me, and would never think that I had to fulfill an unholy purpose for

Him. I made Him the Lord of my life through baptism, and since that day, He has had His rightful place as God in my life. I have no other gods before Him.

Life can be hard. Human nature often drives us to look to other people for what only God can give. I hope and pray you are aware of your need for God; it's a need that every human being has. I also pray you are involved in a vibrant, life-changing personal relationship with Him, because that's where you will find everything you need. If you would like to make Jesus your Lord, Al will lead you through the process at the end of this book. It's the best decision you could ever make!

Chapter 16

THE HEALING BEGINS

"I am the Lord who heals you."

—EXODUS 15:26

AL: For several weeks, I did a lot of thinking and praying about my next steps with Lisa. I sought good advice from people I trusted—and I got a lot of advice from people whose counsel I did not necessarily want. Working in a church can be like living in a fishbowl; everybody wanted to know what I was going to do— some out of concern and some out of curiosity. This was a private matter, for sure, but because of my involvement in leadership in the church, it also had a public element.

I chose to confide in a few close, confidential friends and family members, and to say very little to everyone else. I was not sure what I was going to do, and I did not want to start rumors. I also felt Lisa should be aware of my decision before anyone else knew about it, so I tried to keep the whole situation as quiet as possible. That didn't work very well.

Because of my job at the church, I was accountable to a group of elders. Out of love for Lisa and me and concern for the way our circumstances could impact the church, they decided one night to make a strong suggestion about how I should handle my marriage. They came up with a plan—almost a program for reconciliation, which included sending Lisa to a counseling center for several months. They believed she and I definitely needed to spend some time apart, and they seemed to think some kind of managed relationship, with them as our overseers, was a good idea.

When I heard the elders' recommendation, I realized that they'd based it on their love and friendship for us, but something inside me rose up and said, *No. This is not what we're going to do. These men are not going to dictate how Lisa and I need to deal with our problems.* I respected them and worked well with them in church matters, but when it came to my marriage, I was not going to give them a vote.

From my perspective, the elders' plan was a big overreach of authority. I already felt betrayed by my wife, and now I felt betrayed by my church leaders too. They were supposed to be helping me, but I felt they were imposing their opinions on a very personal matter. On one hand, I was crushed; on the other hand, I wouldn't stand for it.

I called Lisa and asked her to meet me at our house.

Lisa says now that she was terrified to meet me. She had no idea what I would say or do and was afraid I might present her with divorce papers. That was not what I had in mind.

I could tell she was nervous when she arrived for our conversation. We had not spoken at all since she left, except when we needed to talk about the girls. We had not had any discussion at all about the affair, about our present circumstances, or about our future.

I immediately told her what the elders thought we should do and then said, "That's not right. I'm going to resign from the church. I don't know if there is a future for us or not, but I do know it's not going to be decided by anyone but us."

I found out later that my dad, who was also an elder at the church, stood up for me in one of their meetings. He was one of the family members who did not think I should make any effort to restore my marriage, and he shared that with the group. He said, "I'm telling Al to divorce Lisa, but it has to be his decision. This whole proposal is not the right call."

> On one hand, I was crushed; on the other hand, I wouldn't stand for it.

As a result, the elders eventually backed away from their idea, but by that time it did not matter much. I had already decided not to take their advice and had already written my letter of resignation from the church. I did not know how to move forward with Lisa or what I would do without a job; I just knew I had to decide my future for myself. Thankfully, I never had to give them that letter.

FORGIVEN FOREVER

Before I found out about the affair, Lisa and I had arranged a ministry trip to Europe and planned to take the girls with us. Of course, she would not make that trip, but I decided to go ahead. I thought the change of scenery and change of pace would be good for me. I also felt teaching and preaching again would be a positive experience. Besides, I wanted the girls to see Europe. In those days, restrictions on air travel were not as stringent as they are now, so my mom was able to travel with us on Lisa's ticket.

Before we left, Lisa and I had a talk. I had decided that if I could go to Europe for two weeks and not miss her, then I could go on living my life without her. If I did miss her and could keep from being paralyzed by worrying about what she might be doing, I reasoned, then I needed to make an effort to restore our relationship. She had been baptized by then. She did this totally of her own volition; I had nothing to do with it. I did not even know about it when it happened, so she obviously did not do it to gain my approval. I had also heard lots of good reports about positive changes Lisa was making in her life, and I could see firsthand that she was trying to do better. But I still did not trust her. I would just have to wait and see how I felt while I was overseas.

On the flight to Europe, I tried to read a book called *Forgiven Forever* (now titled *Getting Past Guilt*) by Joe Beam. After only reading a few sentences, I felt overwhelmed and closed the book. I was not ready to read it.

When I first stood to preach and teach in Europe, I felt like a shell of a man. As I went on, I could hardly believe the emotion that came rushing out of my heart as I spoke. In addition to

Mom and the girls, several others from our church were on that trip. They seemed to begin to realize that something deep was happening in me, and they rallied around me in support. I began to feel stronger.

I did not want the girls to feel disconnected from their mom while we were away, so I called Lisa several times during the trip so they could talk to her. And I realized I missed her. I also wasn't worried about what she was doing. I had a peace for which I can only give credit to God—a peace that told me that she was finished seeing the man with whom she had been unfaithful to me. By the time the trip was over, about two months after Lisa admitted the affair and I asked her to leave, I knew I wanted to get back together with her.

During our flight home, I picked up Joe Beam's book again and read it completely. In Joe's case, he played the role Lisa played in our marriage, and his wife, Alice, was able to forgive him for his infidelity. Reading about Joe's mind-set through his wandering from God and straying from his wife helped me understand how a person thinks when trapped in sinful behavior. The reality, depth, and power of true forgiveness hit me like a sledgehammer. I realized what forgiveness would look like if I chose to extend it to Lisa. It would not be easy, but I wanted to make the effort.

TRUE FORGIVENESS

Back in West Monroe, Lisa continued to live with John and Paula, but she and I were talking every day, working toward reconciliation. I told her we had to have a fresh start; we needed a clean slate, a complete do-over. We needed to find a new way to have a relationship and a marriage, and I told her I did not want to sleep with her until we both agreed that we were fully reconciled.

> When I forgave Lisa, her affair became off-limits as a weapon in conversations or arguments.

We began our journey toward restoration by going to counseling together and committing to doing what we needed to do—and with a lot of prayer and Bible study.

From a personal perspective, the best thing I was able to do by God's grace was to forgive Lisa *completely*. I learned that people do not really give forgiveness if they do not practice forgiveness day in and day out. For me, practicing forgiveness meant I would never, ever use the affair to hurt her or to hurt us. When I forgave her, it became off-limits as a weapon in conversations and arguments. I could not pretend the affair never happened, but I did have to neutralize its power and refuse to use it against her. I chose to do that, and at the time of this writing, fifteen years later, she would tell you that I have honored that commitment.

Once I chose to truly forgive Lisa, I shared that decision with my family. Interestingly, I allowed her back into my life much more easily than they did. Several of them thought I had made the wrong decision. They felt shut out of my life, to a degree, and maybe they were, because I did not let their opinions influence me. I loved them, but I could not allow them to come between my wife and me if we wanted to be together. And we did want to be together.

Lisa and I took an intensely personal, honest journey toward restoration, and when we decided we were ready, we bought new wedding rings for each other, held a private vow-renewal ceremony in December 1999, and spent our first night together as a newly and truly committed husband and wife.

A New Season

LISA: Once Al and I renewed our vows, our marriage did start over. Getting off to a new beginning was not always easy, but we were committed—even stubborn—about it, so we persevered through the difficult moments. We rebuilt our relationship on godly principles, using the Bible as our authority and guide. We were as open as we felt wisdom allowed us to be with the people of the church and with our families. Most of the people in the church were happy to see us back together and supportive of our reconciliation. Many of the Robertsons, however, were not in favor of our vow renewal, and I knew that. In a way, the fact that Al stood up to them and fought for our marriage against their wishes showed me beyond any shadow of a doubt that he really was committed to our relationship.

Several days after we renewed our vows, the church put on a Christmas play, and lots of Robertsons had roles to play, including me. Korie played Mary, and John Luke was the baby Jesus. Phil played John the Baptist, Al was a disciple, and I was one of the townspeople in Bethlehem. During rehearsals for the play, our family members weren't ugly or rude to me, but we all knew our relationships had been damaged.

Like our play practices, our family Christmas celebration that year was awkward. Again, no one was unkind to me, but I knew—and understood why—they did not trust me. Rebuilding relationships was going to take time, I realized. But I knew these people; I knew I wanted close relationships with them, and I was willing to do whatever it took to earn their trust again and repair the bridges I had burned. As soon as Al and I got back together, I wrote a heartfelt letter of apology to the Robertson family, telling them how sorry I was for the pain I had caused Al, our daughters, and all of them. They accepted the apology, and though rebuilding their trust did take time, we now enjoy fully restored relationships with one another, and I dearly love everyone in the family.

By that time, I had a job at a medical technology office. I was determined to pay back every cent of the money I had embezzled, so every time I got paid, I wrote a check to Duck Commander. After several months, I noticed those checks were not clearing my bank, so I asked Miss Kay about them. I will never forget what she said: "I don't want your money, Lisa. You don't have to keep sending those checks. I'm not going to cash them. Your repentance means more to me than the money does." No one ever has to wonder where Al got his generous, forgiving heart!

Into the next year, Al and I continued counseling, and that proved extremely valuable. I came to understand how much of my sinful behavior was rooted in my experiences with being molested as a child, and I was finally able to forgive the man who hurt me so deeply. Al was able to forgive the guy with whom I had the affair. These two acts of forgiveness were vitally important in our healing then and in the freedom we continue to enjoy today.

SEASONED REFLECTIONS . . .

AL: After I found out about Lisa's affair and began to sort through the feelings of betrayal, rejection, anger, and hurt, I realized I could not let my emotions guide my actions toward Lisa or my thoughts about how we would relate to each other in the future. I only knew one trustworthy source of wisdom and advice—the Word of God. No matter how I felt, I could not deny that the Bible affirms marriage as a permanent union. At first, I struggled to accept what the concept of permanence meant for me on a personal level, but over time, I had to admit something I had known for years—that honoring and obeying God's Word is always the path to blessing. If God says marriage is to be permanent, then I wanted to do everything I could to rebuild my relationship with Lisa, not even allowing something as devastating and serious as infidelity to separate us.

In today's culture, values like loyalty and perseverance are becoming a lost art. If we decide we don't like certain people, we can "unfriend" them at the touch of a button. Some sectors of our society seem to be losing appreciation for longevity in relationships; instead of permanence, many are seeking relationships that are valuable for a season, like when people need a new job or a friend with benefits. We believe these trends are detrimental to people, individually and collectively, and we see them as particularly dangerous to the institution of marriage, which always has been and always will be designed to be permanent and unbreakable.

When the Bible speaks of becoming "one flesh," that's about as permanent an arrangement as anyone could come up with. Of course, this idea includes God's intention of intimacy in a sexual relationship, when two people become one anatomically. It's also the reason behind the tradition of a husband and wife sharing the same last name. When we married, "Al and Lisa" became "the Robertsons."

Once two people have joined their lives together in unity and become one, they become something different than they were before they entered the marriage covenant. Making this unified creation separate again is painful. Think about it: Even something as simple as an apple is one unified object. It cannot be made "two" without cutting. Any time a relationship that is intended to stay together gets separated, neither

> Once two people have joined their lives together in unity, they become something different than they were before they entered the marriage covenant.

person involved can go back to being exactly who they were before the breech. They've become one with someone else, and they cannot simply take back everything they put into the marriage or they will lose part of themselves.

We once visited a beautiful place in Arkansas, a lookout point with gorgeous views of mountains and valleys. We could envision lots of weddings taking place there, with this breathtaking vista as a backdrop. Before we left, we looked down and saw a broken glass container with some sand in it. Immediately, both of us thought we knew what had happened.

In many wedding ceremonies, a bride and groom each pour a small amount of sand, sometimes sands of different colors, into a container and mix it to symbolize their new unity and life together. The point of this gesture is that once grains of sand are mixed, they cannot be separated again. They're together forever.

We will never know for sure how the broken container we saw ended up at the lookout point. The wind had blown away most of the sand, but we could clearly see grains of two colors remaining. Our theory is that someone once got married there, then the marriage went bad, and the person went back to that spot to shatter the glass vessel as a representation of their devastated relationship. When we saw it, we looked at each other with so much sympathy for this couple, whoever they were, and thought about the depths of pain they must have felt.

When we teach or counsel couples, we tell them marriage is a "no surrender, no evacuation" arrangement. We also talk to them about the fact that they cannot just "opt out" of their marriage without severe consequences. The reason a broken marriage is so painful is that marriages were never meant to be torn apart. From the very beginning, God has intended for people to stay together as husband and wife, allowing nothing but death to separate them.

No doubt marriage is an environment in which to make

mistakes, and plenty of mistakes are made. But marriage is also a place to make amends. In a relationship designed to be permanent, grudges and hard-heartedness cannot be allowed. A marriage relationship has to be a place where apologies flow freely. It's a relationship of ultimate accountability and constant forgiveness, and the keys to permanence are honesty and trust. That's the only way to live together forever in peace, joy, and blessing.

Just as a human being is designed to be "one" for life and cannot easily disconnect from an arm or a leg, marriages are also created for unity that lasts a lifetime. A commitment to a husband or wife cannot be viewed as temporary or "until things get really hard" in an ideal marriage. To live under God's blessing, both husband and wife have to understand that it's a permanent arrangement. God knows it will be hard at times. There may even be times when one or both spouses want to leave the marriage. We know what that's like. We also know the rewards that come with choosing to stay together, no matter what difficulties arise. By God's grace and a lot of trust in His ability to heal hurts, habits, and hang-ups, Lisa and I were able to reconcile and not divorce—and what a great thing that has turned out to be!

Chapter 17

WORTH IT

"So I will restore to you the years that the swarming
locust has eaten . . .
You shall eat in plenty and be satisfied,
And praise the name of the Lord your God,
Who has dealt wondrously with you;
And My people shall never be put to shame . . .
I am the Lord your God and there is no other."

—JOEL 2:25–27

LISA: After Al and I renewed our vows, we had a lot to learn. We had already tried to build a marriage our way; we needed to build one God's way. I knew the two of us would have to work together to understand what God wanted from us and for us, but I also knew we both as individuals needed to be sensitive to God's Spirit and follow His leading in our personal lives as He restored our life together.

For me, following God's guidance certainly meant continuing to spend time studying the Bible and praying, participating in church groups, and surrounding myself with godly people who would support my new life. It also meant making some big changes on a practical level. For many years, actually until Al and I renewed our marriage, my outward appearance said more about my inner struggles and realities than words could ever say. I did not dress modestly at all. In fact, as I mentioned in the "Seasoned Reflections" section of chapter 12, I usually wore tight-fitting clothes, short skirts, and low necklines. I also wore way too much makeup. Generally speaking, I looked provocative. I also carried myself in ways I thought would be attractive to men, spoke to men in certain tones of voice, and hugged them just a little too long and a little too tightly. Before I truly surrendered my life to Christ, these things seemed to be part of my persona. I did not realize they were inappropriate.

Once Jesus became Lord of my life, one of the quick lessons He taught me was that I needed to dress, speak, and act differently. Almost immediately, I wanted men to see me only as Al's wife or as a sister in Christ—nothing more, ever. I started wearing higher necklines and lower hemlines; I toned down my makeup and learned to interact with men appropriately and modestly. These outward adjustments reflected the deep, thorough internal changes God was working in my heart. He gave me the knowledge of what I needed to do, and I did it. Al says now that he could hardly believe how much and how quickly I changed. He never said a word to me about my appearance. He simply allowed God to lead me and gave me the freedom to follow.

SLAYING A GIANT

AL: After Lisa and I recommitted our marriage to God, both of us began to change. Lisa has described some of the changes she went through, and I learned to be more sensitive to her needs and more emotionally available. I also learned to balance marriage, family, and ministry in a healthier way. My being away on ministry trips for days and sometimes weeks was tough on Lisa, so I decided that any invitation I received had to include her or I simply would not accept it. This decision turned out to be great for my confidence, for her confidence, and for the churches and mission organizations we visited.

Many times, when the enemy has wreaked havoc in people's lives and God begins to turn things around for them, something from the past crops up to threaten their progress. Lisa and I were no exception to that. One day, we had several errands to run, including one to our local Walmart. Without warning, I noticed that Lisa grew stiff in the seat beside me and said, "Let's go home." That made no sense to me at all.

When I asked her what was wrong, she said the man with whom she had the affair was two cars in front of us, also turning into the Walmart parking lot. I had to make a decision right then. Would we run the risk of facing him in Walmart, or would we avoid him? I pulled into the next available parking space, roiling inside, and said to Lisa, "We're going to walk into Walmart and buy the things we came to get. You are going to hold your head

> "You chose me, and I chose you. And we are not going to live in fear of anyone in our own hometown."

high, and so am I. You chose me, and I chose you. And we are not going to live in fear of anyone in our own hometown."

Lisa was uncomfortable, of course, but she agreed. In the store, we ended up buggy to buggy with that man and his female companion. As soon as they recognized us, they wheeled that buggy around like the store was on fire and practically ran away from us. That moment was such a triumph for us. We faced a fear, and it cowered. It wasn't easy; it took all the strength we had. But it was worth it.

That experience helped us understand that any reconciliation will be tested, especially early on, when people's hearts are still so sensitive and vulnerable. Since that day, we have never looked back and have enjoyed constant growth and increasing intimacy in our relationship.

SEEDS FOR THE FUTURE

Our church held a marriage retreat in the spring of 2000. One of the leaders invited us, and the church paid our way. At that time, we were still very tender emotionally, feeling like newborn colts taking their first wobbly steps. It was a great time of listening, learning, and healing. The other people in the group treated us wonderfully, and the whole weekend was a great experience. In addition to giving us just what we needed that weekend, God planted in our hearts some important marriage principles for our future—not just for us, but for countless other couples we would encounter in the years to come.

As we soaked in biblical teachings about marriage and as other couples encouraged us while on the retreat, I could not help thinking about everything Lisa and I had learned through our own difficulties. Even though our situation was still fairly recent, I was filled with a desire to help people who were discouraged or ready to give up on their relationships with their spouses. I also knew Lisa and I needed, but had not yet regained, enough credibility to start ministering to people.

A little more than a year after we reconciled, in the spring of 2000, Lisa and I were still in counseling and reached a point where our therapist felt we were ready to move forward without her. We knew she would always be there if we needed her, but completing those months of counseling was a milestone for us. We had done some hard work—some of it grueling and emotionally excruciating—but we had grown as individuals and as a couple through all of it. We were so happy to start walking on our own.

The church held another marriage retreat the following spring, in 2001, and asked Lisa and me to plan and host our version of *The Newlywed Game*. I planned the questions and served as the host, and Lisa played the role of Vanna White. We had fun doing that, but on a deeper level, we really appreciated being asked. It was the first time anyone had invited us to do anything regarding marriage in any kind of leadership capacity, even if it was a takeoff on a game show. That opportunity communicated to us that our church had also healed from the trauma of the affair, and just as we chose to make a fresh start, they were also willing to let us begin again and not hold the past against us.

By this time, the authenticity and solidity of our renewed relationship was evident, and people began pulling us aside, telling us their marriage troubles, and asking, "How did you get through that? What can you tell us to help us survive what we're going through right now and keep our marriage together?" Others called us and asked if we would meet with them and help them through a particular problem in their marriage. In addition to that, young engaged couples began asking us to do their premarital counseling. In an informal, organic kind of way, we eventually found ourselves the go-to couple for marriages in crisis.

For several years after those first two marriage retreats, we continued to provide leadership to the marriage retreat, eventually helping plan it and then hosting the entire event. Since then, we have had more and more opportunities to help people whose marriages are suffering—through teaching classes at our church, counseling with individuals or couples, speaking at seminars, or ministering in churches. We have shared everything we know that might help restore a damaged relationship. We have been determined not to hold back the shameful aspects of our pasts because we realize that our courage to talk about the difficult matters gives other people courage to talk about their difficult matters too. We never had anything to offer except what we had learned on our journey, and we have shared our story openly and tried to pass along to others the wisdom and insights God has given us. People have responded well, and we are so thankful to see how God has used our past pain to help and strengthen others.

OUR REWARD

LISA: Al and I have an amazing relationship today. We live with a degree of love and intimacy with each other that we once thought was not even a remote possibility. We have a completely open, trusting relationship characterized by mutual respect and honor. After all we have been through, we do not take each other for granted, and we speak freely about our love and commitment to one another. God has blessed us with the opportunity to spend much time together, and we truly enjoy each other's company. And on top of all that, we have lots of fun with each other and with our family.

In addition to the relationship Al and I now enjoy with each other, being able to help other couples has been extremely fulfilling for Al and me. When we see a husband and wife struggling with some of the same issues we have dealt with, we appreciate being able to relate to them and letting them know we really do understand. If we can help one family avoid the hurt we have suffered, then our pain serves a redemptive purpose. Beyond the redemption we have experienced in our lives and have been privileged to help others experience, we also enjoy what we consider a great reward in the wake of all the drama of our past. Let me explain.

Hebrews 10:35–36 says: "Therefore do not cast away your confidence, which has great reward. For you have need of endurance, so that after you have done the will of God, you may receive the promise." Al and I believe that staying together after infidelity was God's will for us and that we are now reaping some of the blessings and rewards of doing so. Our rewards are our happily married daughters and our grandchildren. When we look at Carley, Bailey, Corban, and Sage we see the fruit that our ultimate decision to remain faithful to one another has produced. We had no idea, when we were trying to decide what to do in 1999, what we would have missed had we chosen to go our separate ways.

> We had no idea, when we were trying to decide what to do in 1999, what we would have missed had we chosen to go our separate ways.

Our family gives us the greatest joys we know. For all the pain we suffered at one season in our lives, we now feel we have received exponential happiness in return. When we spend time with our family, having fun together and listening to children laugh and play, Al and I often look at each other to silently say, *This is worth everything we suffered.* When we think about the fact that we stayed together and realize that our children and grandchildren have been spared the pain of a divorce between us, we thank God. We know we have given our daughters, our sons-in-law, and our grandchildren a legacy of love that is both tender and tough—a legacy of trust in God through the most difficult circumstances, and a legacy of faithfulness to God and to each other. Our journey has not been easy, but if everything we suffered was necessary in order to get us to the point in life where we are now, it was worth it.

SEASONED REFLECTIONS . . .

LISA: I know we have imparted a lot of information in the preceding chapters and that we have been especially forthright about our struggles. We have done this to encourage you. If we can't tell other people how God has healed us and made us whole again, we give Satan a foothold.

Jesus died on a cross for you, me, Al, everyone who reads this book—and everyone who does not read it. Everyone. Part of our responsibility to Him is to tell those who don't know what He has done about His finished work on the cross. We have dedicated our lives to seeking Him and allowing Him to heal us. As that happens, we want to talk about it, share it with others, write about it—spread the good news every way we can. We do not do this to "toot our horn" but to bring others to Christ. We have a burning on the inside of us to show others that they too can be healed by His grace, His forgiveness, and His perfect sacrifice.

My last piece of advice would be this: whatever your struggle is, confess it, own it, and allow God to heal you so you can move on into all the great things He has for you. How effective will you be in God's kingdom if you live as a victim, hoping each day might be your last and never being able to share your struggles and triumphs? If you need to find a group of people who are open to mistakes, do it. Don't stay with any group where you cannot admit problems and find relief and freedom from your sins.

One program that has a great success rate for helping hurting people is Celebrate Recovery, and there are many Celebrate Recovery groups that meet in cities and towns throughout the United States. You can just Google Celebrate Recovery to find a group meeting near you. Some people may think this program is only for alcoholics and drug addicts, but Al and I say it's for "life addicts." People who say they don't have a hurt, habit, or hang-up in life are blessed, but chances are they are not being truthful. All of us have been lost at some point, but Jesus came to seek and save the lost. His sacrifice reaches beyond race, gender, ethnicity, socio-economic obstacles, and political barriers—and it is for you. Don't let your life send a message of hopelessness. Let God help you to be full of hope, healing, and joy!

God bless you for reaching out to God and for reading our book.

AL: Writing this book has been an emotional journey for Lisa and me. We do not glory in our past mistakes or fail-ures. Our story is painful, and parts of it are still hard for us to talk about. Though Lisa and I have both forgiven each other and ourselves, and though we know God has forgiven us, I am ashamed of eighteen-year-old Al. I still lament not being more committed to Christ as a teenager and as a young man, not getting more involved in my church youth group, and making bad decisions. I could have chosen to do so many things the right way, but I chose the wrong way. Sometimes I wonder how different Lisa's life would have been had I been a better person. I thank God for the way He has redeemed my life, for the ways He has changed me, and for the grace He continues to bless me with every day.

Like me, plenty of other people have made mistakes—some of them with severe consequences. If I could put all of those people in a duck blind and talk to them for a few minutes, I would emphasize that the past can be forgiven and redeemed. No matter what has happened, God always offers a second chance. And I hope those people would take me seriously because I am living proof that second chances exist.

I thank God for giving me a second chance to love and serve Him after my time in New Orleans and for giving me a second chance to love Lisa and have her love me. She is one of the strongest, most loving, most committed people I have ever met. There is no limit to the love and respect I have for her.

In the wake of Lisa's affair, my brother Jase wrote me a letter. I won't share the details of it, but I will say that he did not think I should rebuild my relationship with Lisa. About a year after Lisa and I were reconciled and Lisa's relationships with my whole family were restored, we went to church one Sunday night when Jase was preaching. He started his sermon by saying he wanted to talk about three of the most godly women in his life. He first spoke about his wife, Missy. Then he talked about our mom, Miss Kay. Then, to our total shock, he began to share some things about Lisa. Lisa and I both burst into tears. I view that moment as one of the most powerful times in the life of our family. After all Lisa had been through with men, the fact that a man (Jase) would stand up in front of an audience and praise her spiritual courage and call her a godly woman had a profound effect on her. Through Jase, I felt she was finally being recognized for the woman God made her to be, the woman she fought to become.

Lisa and I have made a conscious decision not to allow past mistakes to dictate our present and future lives. We make that decision afresh every single day. This takes discipline and trust in a power far greater than we are.

Many who are trying to reconcile after infidelity have asked me, "How can you ever really trust again?" This is a valid question. I admit that there will always be some doubts. My answer is that God revealed the dishonesty once, and I found out what was going on. I trust that if something like that ever happens again, He will come through again. This is what I tell those who ask—and it's what I tell myself. I also encourage people to trust God first and then trust their spouse. So far, that has worked well for me.

> The fact that a man (Jase) would stand up in front of an audience and praise Lisa's spiritual courage and call her a godly woman had a profound effect on her.

Lisa and I also try to live Paul's words to the Philippian church in Philippians 2:3–4: "Do nothing out of selfish ambition or vain conceit. Rather, in humility value others above yourselves, not looking to your own interests but each of you to the interests of the others." We try to always put the other's interests ahead of our own and it is working beautifully!

Chapter 18

FUTURE SEASONS

Forgetting what is behind and straining toward
what is ahead, I press on toward the goal to win
the prize for which God has called me heavenward
in Christ Jesus.

—PHILIPPIANS 3:13–14 (NIV 2011)

AL: One way Lisa and I have always been able to cope with some of the difficult times in our life and marriage is to see the potential end to those trying days. We also have the same approach to the enjoyable times, as well, knowing they will not always last. We call them seasons. There was the season of being newly married, the season of having and raising our children, the season of discontent in our marriage, the season of teenage daughters, the seasons of career and job changes, the wedding seasons, grandchildren seasons, and on and on. Solomon thought of this well before we did, when he wrote Ecclesiastes 3, and a band called the Byrds sang about it with a smash hit the year I was born in 1965: to everything, there is a season to either endure or enjoy.

OUR CURRENT SEASON

The season Lisa and I find ourselves in now is an exciting one. We are praying and planning on our marriage being strong, being healthy, and growing until one of us goes home to be with the Lord. We are experiencing tremendous thrills with the coming of our grandchildren, and that season seems to be far too short. We are launching into a new season professionally as well.

After twenty-two years in full-time ministry at our home church, White's Ferry Road Church, Lisa and I left our jobs at the church in 2012 to rejoin Duck Commander, and particularly the Robertson family's hit television show, *Duck Dynasty*. We have also helped with book deals and compiled *The Duck Commander Devotional*, and Lisa coauthored *The Women of Duck Commander*.

The time Lisa and I have been able to spend with my family has been a tremendous blessing to us. We travel a lot with Mom and Dad and thoroughly enjoy getting to spend so much time with them. We bought a house on the same street as Willie and Jase, and then Jep followed suit and bought one on that street as well. For the first time since Lisa and I and my baby daughters left our house on the river in 1989 halfway through preaching school, the four brothers are living together in the same neighborhood.

We enter one another's houses as if they were our own, and my brothers' children play together with my grandchildren most days. We eat a lot of meals together, work together filming the show, appear together at events around the country, and attend church together when we are home. We also fuss sometimes, get on each other's nerves, and have to apologize and forgive each other. We live in both an ideal and real world with our family. We are not perfect, but we all have given our lives to a perfect Savior, which makes things work very well for us.

Lisa and I first came to *Duck Dynasty* as fans of the show, like everyone else. We sat on the sidelines for the first year watching the show and enjoying it like so many others. We loved the show for the same reasons others did; it was funny and folksy and ultimately had a message that was positive and a spiritual component that was subtle but definitely recognizable, especially when compared to other reality-type shows. The show was marketed the first season with the tagline "Money, Family, and Ducks." We changed that tagline to "Faith, Family, and Ducks," and that has been our creed ever since.

> My brothers and I enter one another's houses as if they were our own, and their children play with my grandchildren most days.

We don't believe it was an accident that our show became a big hit and that our family has been so well recognized around the world. The team at A&E network did a masterful job at getting the beards and their wives out there in the public eye, but once they were known, would there be anything of substance to make people want to know them better? I was present when the first family dinner scene was filmed for the pilot episode, and I remember clearly Dad's saying that we always pray before we eat a meal together. Because that was a regular and very important part of our family tradition, it became a part of the show and, ultimately, the reason that so many have connected to the show and to our family.

A HERITAGE OF FAITH

My grandparents on my father's side were wonderful Christians who raised their seven children to follow their example of faith. All of my uncles and aunts from the Robertson family have a special place in my heart. They are people of tremendous strength and faith. Two have gone home to be with the Lord, but I am so grateful for their example. Six out of seven of the Robertson children became strong Christians; only one—my dad—strayed from the path and became a prodigal son for ten years.

My mom became a Christian at the age of twenty-six, because the hard life she was living with my wayward dad offered daily misery and little hope. A year later, my dad followed my mom in faith and submitted his will to Christ. At twenty-eight years old, the prodigal son returned to the fold in a dramatic and powerful way. Mom and Dad caught fire for the Lord, and that flame still burns bright after forty years of service! As we have written earlier in this book, Lisa and I eventually made that same decision to follow Christ after a lot of hardheaded, hard-hearted living and wrong choices. My children have made the same decision, and all of my brothers and their wives and now some of their older children are followers of Christ too.

Our faith in Christ is not only the bond that holds our family together, but we believe it is the reason we have been raised up, recognized, and given the opportunity to appear on television, write books, and speak to hundreds of thousands of people. We have a story to tell that can transform individuals, families, cultures, and eternal destinies. The story comes from the Holy Bible, and it has been rescuing people for thousands of years.

THE STORY THAT NEVER ENDS

When the very first wife and the very first husband, Adam and Eve, broke the one command that God had given them, sin was unleashed into the human race (Genesis 3). Their relationship with God would never be the same, nor would their relationship with each other. More bad choices were made, and more sin was committed, and from the first couple right up until today, sin has been present, and it continues to destroy relationships. God told Adam and Eve that they would die because of sin and they did, both spiritually, in terms of their relationship to God, and physically, when they were cast out of the garden and forbidden to eat of the tree of life.

When you and I first had an awareness of our sin, by choosing to break a command of God, we suffered the same fate as the original couple and every person who has ever lived since. The Bible tells us in Romans 3:23 that all have sinned and fallen short of the glory of God. Because of that sin, we lose forever a permanent relationship with God. And since we will die physically one day, because of sin, we lose the hope of ever living beyond the years we have here on earth. Another problem with sin is that it provides a miserable existence for the years we do have here on earth. Lisa and I have described many of the miseries from our past life, and there aren't enough trees on earth to provide paper to write all of the terrible things that people do to themselves and to others because of sinful choices and behaviors. Sin is devastating, destructive, and damning.

Thankfully, the Creator of the cosmos said in John 3:16–17, "For God so loved the world that he gave his one and only Son, that whoever believes in him shall not perish but have eternal life. For God did not send his Son into the world to condemn the world, but to save the world through him" (NIV 2011).

> God knew we would choose to disobey and suffer the consequences, so He had a plan to save us from ourselves and our sins.

God knew we would choose to disobey and suffer the consequences, so He had a plan to save us from ourselves and our sins. His plan was that God would become a man, not by natural ways, but in a supernatural way, to offer Himself as a sacrifice large enough for all of human sin.

A virgin girl named Mary conceived a child, not with a man, but by the power of the Holy Spirit. Her son, Jesus of Nazareth, grew into a man and proclaimed Himself the Son of God who had come to give His life for the sins of all mankind. He claimed that His death on a Roman cross of execution would allow all sinners the choice to call on Him, instead of their own merit, to repair their damaged relationship with God. His death would provide anyone the opportunity to choose something larger than their own weaknesses and sinful choices.

After Jesus' death, He was buried in a tomb. But after three days, He arose from the dead and appeared to hundreds of people before levitating out of sight, into the heavens, proclaiming that He would return one day to gather all of those who call on Him (John 20–21; Acts 1:1–11). Jesus' resurrection and ascension give hope beyond the grave and beyond sin's ability to continually weaken all humanity. Because He rose, there is hope that we can live beyond our deaths, which were caused by sin. Because He lives, there is hope for a more abundant life while here on earth. Sin is still present, but it does not have to control our lives or our eternal destiny.

Peter, one of Jesus' close friends and disciples during His life on earth, wrote these words of encouragement in 1 Peter 1:3–5: "Praise be to the God and Father of our Lord Jesus Christ! In his great mercy he has given us new birth into a living hope through the resurrection of Jesus Christ from the dead, and into an inheritance that can never perish, spoil or fade. This inheritance is kept in heaven for you, who through faith are shielded by God's power until the coming of the salvation that is ready to be revealed in the last time" (NIV 2011). That same Peter taught the first-ever gospel message of salvation in Acts 2. He told some of the very ones who had nailed Jesus to a cross that redemption and forgiveness for sin were available by embracing and submitting to Jesus Christ. About three thousand people were cut to the heart by that message and believed in Jesus' sacrifice. They confessed their allegiance and were baptized in water to show their submission to Him, and they received a wonderful gift of the Holy Spirit to help guide them as they lived out their years helping others, pointing people to eternal life, and raising the quality of their own lives and the lives of their families.

A NEW SEASON . . .

AL: I believe with all of my heart that the story of salvation recorded in the Bible is the absolute truth and is available for all men and women. Lisa and I did the same thing the people did on the Day of Pentecost in Acts 2—exactly what many others recorded in the book of Acts and throughout ancient and modern history for the past two thousand years have done. We know the devastating nature of serving sin and serving ourselves. We have been there and done that! We also know the cleansing and freeing nature of following Christ, living with the help of the Holy Spirit, and understanding forgiveness, redemption, and renewal. Atheism and many of the world's religions offer no hope of escaping sin's wrath, no hope beyond a certain grave, and no hope of deliverance from the misery of humanity's bad behavior.

Lisa and I don't look back at how our sinfulness damaged us; instead we look ahead to the promise of eternity together with God. I would not have known how to deal with my own weaknesses or Lisa's weaknesses had I not had help recognizing the true nature of sin and its consequences. Faith in Christ, the Bible, and people who have lived and learned helped show us a better way. If you are living an unfulfilled life because of your sin or someone else's sin, we offer you the first step to healing and hope.

Anything we could tell you by way of advice for your life or marriage would begin with asking you if you have embraced Christ as your Savior. The salvation we received from Christ was our first step to a better life, a better way of thinking, and a better way of handling the effects of sin and its consequences.

How do you embrace Christ as your Savior? Believe that Jesus is who He says He is. Look at how many have been blessed by believing! Tell Him you will follow Him, learn more about Him, and tell others about Him. Commit yourself to following His example of living. Read His story, the Bible, and be ready to have a blessed and fulfilled life (John 10:8–10). Show the world you really have submitted your will to Him by being baptized to reenact His death, burial, and resurrection in that watery grave (Romans 6:1–14).

Once you are a Christian, the fruit that will begin to come forth from your life will be different. It will be fruit that is Spirit driven and not sin driven. Your life, your marriage, and your family will be better than you could have ever imagined (Galatians 5:16–26).

Lisa and I live a redeemed life, free from our past sins and hurts. We are deeply in love with our God and with each other. We love our children and grandchildren, and we know we are providing stability for them and a legacy of hope and truth, and an ability to handle whatever crisis comes their way—and the crises will come! Our new season is rich in love and mercy and is providing us with joy in all circumstances. We pray the same for the next season of your life, marriage, and family.

TWO KEYS TO A DYNAMIC MARRIAGE

AL: I mentioned Genesis 2:24–25 earlier in this book and called attention to the fact that it points us to what I call the four pillars of an ideal marriage: severance, unity, permanence, and intimacy. Another Scripture passage I believe is equally important is Ephesians 5:21–33, and it contains two of the best secrets I know for a happy marriage. What are they? To be lovable and respectable.

I want to call your attention to two specific verses in Ephesians 5:21–33. First, notice that verses 22–24 say, "Wives, submit to your husbands as to the Lord. For the husband is the head of the wife, as also Christ is head of the church; and He is the Savior of the body. Therefore, just as the church is subject to Christ, so let the wives be to their own husbands in everything."

Then verse 25 says, "Husbands, love your wives, just as Christ also loved the church and gave Himself for her." And verse 28 says, "So husbands ought to love their own wives as their own bodies; he who loves his wife loves himself."

If wives are to respect their husbands, then husbands need to be respectable. If husbands are to love their wives, then wives need to be lovable. Pretty simple—at least in theory. But how do husbands become respectable and wives become lovable in practical ways?

SEVEN WAYS TO BE RESPECTABLE

I could hardly believe what I saw when I read Job 31:1–30 with the aim of learning to be more respectable. This rarely cited passage is full of insights and teaching that will help a man become a more respectable husband. Because the text is lengthy, I encourage you to read it for yourself in your own Bible or online. For our purposes here, let me highlight seven principles of respectability for you.

1. Protect your eyes and your mind. I cannot overemphasize the importance of being very careful about what you watch and look at and about what you think about. Job says, "I made a covenant with my eyes not to look lustfully at a girl" (verse 1, NIV).

2. Walk in honesty. Throughout this book, the consequences of secrets and dishonesty have been clear. Honesty is nonnegotiable for a happy marriage. Job 31:5–6 says, "If I have walked in falsehood or my foot has hurried after deceit—let God weigh me in honest scales and he will know that I am blameless" (NIV).

3. Protect faithfulness. The marriage relationship is protected and sustained by faithfulness. Lisa and I could have been spared so much heartache had unfaithfulness never entered our lives. Job says, "If my heart has been enticed by a woman, or if I have lurked at my neighbor's door, then may my wife grind another man's grain, and may other men sleep with her" (verses 9–10, NIV).

4. Treat others respectfully. Job offers a great foundation for respecting others when he asks some important questions in verses 13–15: "If I have denied justice to my menservants and maidservants when they had a grievance against me, what will I do when God confronts me? What will I answer when called to account? Did not he who made me in the womb make them? Did not the same one form us both within our mothers?" (NIV). If you want to be a respectable person, always remember that no one is higher or better than anyone else. God made us all!

5. Display consistent generosity. In the midst of a discourse on things he considers negative, Job says, "If I have denied the desires of the poor or let the eyes of the widow grow weary, if I have kept my bread to myself, not sharing it with the fatherless . . . then let my arm fall from the shoulder, let it be broken off at the joint" (verses 16–17 and 22, NIV). I agree with Job. Being selfish is negative, and it can be devastating to a marriage. I am thankful to have been raised by loving, generous people and to have been surrounded by generosity all of my life. Be generous to your spouse first and then to others. That's a great way to live a blessed life.

6. Encourage contentment and refuse to be greedy. People in Job's day struggled just as much as people today with the love of money and with finding security in possessions or finances. Job says, "If I have put my trust in gold or said to pure gold, 'You are my security' . . . then these also would be sins to be judged, for I would have been unfaithful to God on high (verses 24 and 28, NIV). Greed is like selfishness, and it will also destroy a marriage relationship. In 1 Timothy 6:6, Paul writes, "Godliness with contentment is great gain." In other words, do you want to do something great for your marriage and yourself? Follow God and be content.

7. Be forgiving instead of vengeful. Job says, "I have not allowed my mouth to sin by invoking a curse against [my enemy's] life" (verse 30, NIV). I have had to learn a lot of lessons about being a forgiving person—not only by not speaking against people who have done me wrong, but by not allowing my heart to hold grudges or fall into bitterness. I will admit that it's not easy. Sometimes it's very painful. But it's worth it.

SEVEN WAYS TO BE LOVABLE

LISA: Proverbs 31 is often used to describe a godly woman, but I like to call it "the lovability text." If we look closely at its principles, we see seven ways to become wives who are easy for our husbands to love.

1. Build confidence in your husband. When Proverbs 31 describes a godly wife, verse 11 says: "Her husband has full confidence in her" (NIV). I am grateful to be able to say that Al has full confidence in me now, but there were years in our marriage when I gave him no reason at all to be confident in me. In fact, my decisions broke down his confidence in me. If you want to build a happy marriage, give your husband every reason to trust you and be confident in you, then help him build confidence in himself by praising and encouraging him.

2. Bring good, not harm. As a godly wife relates to her husband, "she brings him good, not harm, all the days of her life" (verse 12, NIV). I have firsthand experience with bringing harm to my husband, but those days are over. Now I do everything within my power to bring good to Al in every possible way, even if I have to sacrifice something I want. Wives who bring harm to their husbands can end up destroying marriages and families, so be committed to bringing positive experiences first to your husband and then to everyone else around you.

3. Work to strengthen your household. Let's face it. Running a household and raising a family sometimes feels like running a multinational corporation. There's a *lot* to it! But Proverbs 31:13 says a godly wife "works with eager hands" (NIV). In other words, she embraces the opportunity to bless those in her household, not passing off responsibilities but working hard to keep the household peaceful and pleasant.

4. Manage your family well. The Proverbs 31 woman "gets up while it is still dark; she provides food for her family" (verse 15, NIV). While this verse is certainly true literally at times, it also represents a woman who is sacrificial in her love and care for her family. Whatever they need, she bends over backward to provide.

5. *Extend compassion.* Being a busy wife and mother sometimes seems to require all of our physical and emotional resources, but we need to step outside our own familiar circles at times and remember people in need. Proverbs 31:20 describes an excellent wife as one who "opens her arms to the poor and extends her hands to the needy" (verse 20, NIV). Extending this kind of compassion not only assists those in need, it also helps us remember how blessed we are.

6. *Maintain a sense of humor.* Proverbs 31:25 says a godly woman "can laugh at the days to come" (NIV), and Proverbs 17:22 says, "A merry heart does good, like medicine." In other words, light-heartedness and a good sense of humor will go a long way in a relationship. I have never met a man who likes a nagging, complaining wife who speaks negatively all the time. If you'll be cheerful and find the humor in as many things as possible, that positive attitude will have a beneficial effect on your husband and your home.

7. *Fear the Lord.* Proverbs 31 begins to bring its description of a godly wife to a close with these words: "Charm is deceptive, and beauty is fleeting; but a woman who fears the Lord is to be praised" (NIV). There is no substitute for fearing (giving awesome reverence and respect to) the Lord and for allowing Him to lead you in your relationship with your husband. Had I feared the Lord at various critical moments in my life, I would have made

much better decisions and spared myself and others much pain. But I did not know that then. I do know it now, and I also know that "the fear of the Lord is the beginning of knowledge" (Proverbs 1:7). I cannot imagine a husband who would not treasure, admire, and cherish a wise, God-fearing wife!

ADVICE FOR HUSBANDS AND WIVES

AL: The apostle Paul offers Christians great advice on all kinds of situations. Lisa and I believe that his words in Philippians 2:1–5 provide some of the best guidelines for marriage we have ever seen. We do our very best to live by these words every day, and we pray you will too. If husbands and wives can relate to each other according to these instructions, they will lay a foundation for a happy marriage characterized by love and respect.

> *If you have any encouragement from being united with Christ, if any comfort from his love, if any fellowship with the Spirit, if any tenderness and compassion, then make my joy complete by being like-minded, having the same love, being one in spirit and purpose. Do nothing out of selfish ambition or vain conceit, but in humility consider others better than yourselves. Each of you should look not only to your own interests, but also to the interests of others. Your attitude should be the same as that of Christ Jesus.*

> **—PHILIPPIANS 2:1–5, NIV**

CHAPTER 1

1. When you look back on your childhood, can you think of a person (someone like Al's neighbors or a friend, teacher, or family member) who was a good influence? How did this person affect you?

2. Have you had an experience that you thought was horrible at the time, but later things worked out? How can you see God's hand in your life through those circumstances?

3. God always has a big picture in mind. If you are going through a difficult time right now, will you trust God to see you through it and ultimately work all things together for your good? What steps of trust do you need to take so that God can work in you?

4. How can you apply Al's encouragement to a situation in your life? "I am living proof that bad beginnings can lead to happy endings . . . Stay close to God, persevere through the hard times, and believe life can be better—and pretty soon it will be."

CHAPTER 2

1. Can you relate to some of the hardships Al describes in this chapter? (For example, being abandoned, being poor, being exposed to bad or inappropriate behavior, carrying responsibility at a young age.) How did you feel then, and how do you feel about those situations now?

2. Do you believe God can drastically change a person, like He changed Al's dad, Phil? Why or why not? If you are struggling to believe, what can you do?

3. Have you experienced a turnaround from a bad situation, or are you still waiting for good to come out of it? What areas are you still working on?

4. How can you apply to your life Al's statement "No matter what has happened to you, what other people may have done to you, or what you have done to yourself, your past does not have to determine your future"?

5. Do you know someone for whom change seems impossible? How can you pray for that person, believing that God can completely transform their life?

CHAPTER 3

1. Lisa talks about the sexual abuse she suffered as a child. Have you, or anyone you know, experienced abuse? (It could be psychological, emotional, verbal, physical, or sexual abuse.) What were the effects of that abuse?

2. Why is it hard to get rid of guilt and shame for things we have kept secret?

3. If you have been abused, do you ever wish you had confronted your abuser, as Lisa did? It's not too late to do that with the help of a wise, trusted counselor or therapist. If the abuser is deceased, consider writing him or her a letter. The person will never read it, but putting your feelings on paper could be very healing for you.

4. What do you think is the first step an abused person can take toward healing?

5. How does Lisa's following statement give you hope for your own life or for someone you love? "The wall of shame so many abuse victims feel they must hide behind is coming down . . . The journey to healing is not easy, but it's worth it—and it can happen in your life."

CHAPTER 4

1. How did Lisa's abuse impact the way she thought about herself and her purpose in life? Has anything had that same kind of effect on you?

2. What does intimacy look like to you?

3. Why do you think God's plan for sex is that it be limited to marriage? What happens when people go outside of His plan?

4. If you have failed or made mistakes in some area of your life, including the sexual part, is it too late for restoration? Why or why not? Read what Al says about this and think about how it applies to your life: "Lisa and I both have a history of sexual sin. (Which means we're familiar with all the reasons and excuses for not following God's plan. Been there. Done that.) But we also have a history of forgiveness and redemption, and we know that no matter who you are or what you've done, new beginnings are always an option."

CHAPTER 5

1. What two behaviors that stem from sexual abuse does Lisa describe? What attitudes or behaviors did you have as a teenager that turned out to be unhealthy? What lessons have you learned since that time, and how have you changed and grown?

2. What should a young person do if he or she was caught in a destructive web like Al or Lisa?

3. Al says, "No matter what you have done in your life, no matter how foolish you have been or how many stupid mistakes you have made (and I made plenty!), every day is a new opportunity to choose to be wise and to live in wisdom for the rest of your life." Is it ever too late for a person to choose to live wisely? Why or why not? What wise choice toward change do you need to make today?

4. Lisa writes, "Had we built our relationship on a solid foundation, we most likely would have avoided much of the heartache we have endured." How does a couple build a solid foundation?

CHAPTER 6

1. In what ways does forgiveness change the forgiver as well as the offender?

2. How do you move on when you have been hurt badly?

3. Al's parents showed him "tough love." What is tough love, and how do you express it?

4. Has anyone ever shown you the kind of love Phil showed Al when he returned from New Orleans? How did that make a difference in your life?

5. Al writes*:* "Rebellious young people are often deeply afraid and sometimes ashamed of their behavior once they realize what they've done. When they can also recognize how much they're loved, they have a much easier time changing their ways and learning to make good decisions." When someone you care about wants to make the right choices, why should you be loving instead of judgmental?

CHAPTER 7

1. You may or may not have been involved with a physical abortion, but what plans, hopes, dreams, or relationships have been cut short in your life? What hope did this chapter give you for the fulfillment of those things that have been lost in your life?

2. Lisa tried to fill the hole in her heart with people and behavior that didn't satisfy her longings. Why do you think her attempt to look for love in all the wrong places failed? What or who can truly satisfy?

3. Lisa writes, "The sacrifice of Christ is enough. It's enough to heal you, set you free, restore and redeem your life, and move you toward a greater purpose and destiny than you ever dreamed possible." What does this statement mean to you? Why?

4. If you have a hard time forgiving yourself, ask yourself the same question Lisa asks: "If Jesus can forgive you, why can't you forgive yourself?"

5. Think about Miss Kay's advice: "Confess it. Own it. And move on." What do you need to confess? How do you own it? What practical steps can you take to move on?

6. Reread what Lisa says about Jesus Christ. How did her relationship with Him help Lisa and heal her injured heart? Is it possible for Jesus to do the same for you? If you are not sure, you can invite Him into your life and ask Him to bring restoration and peace to your heart. Al will help you know how to do this in chapter 18.

CHAPTER 8

1. In what specific ways did Al change? What would you like to see change in yourself, and how does Al's life inspire you?

2. When you have been disappointed again and again, how hard is it to accept that a person has been transformed? What difference does Jesus Christ make?

3. What do you think is the most important thing in a marriage relationship?

4. In a letter, Lisa gives her daughter the marriage advice she wishes she'd had: "You can both protect yourselves from the really harmful mistakes by guarding your hearts, your minds, and your marriage. To do this, Christ has to be the center of your life. He has to be the third strand that makes your rope unbreakable."

How does a person go about making Jesus Christ central in a relationship, and why is this so important?

CHAPTER 9

1. Can you picture Al's family on the way to the wedding standing by their disabled car? What mistakes have you made that seem funny to you now?

2. In your own words, what does it mean to "leave and cleave"?

3. Al and Lisa say, "The idea of severance is emotional and mental as much as it is physical. It's essential that we change our allegiance and shuffle our priorities. Even good relationships with parents, siblings, in-laws, and extended family need to take second place to the marriage relationship." What are some practical ways a couple can reprioritize relationships and bond with each other?

4. What is the best way to handle differences between you and your spouse?

CHAPTER 10

1. Al and Lisa found a creative way to be alone when they were living with Granny and Pa. Think of a challenge you are facing

right now, whether it is huge or tiny. How can you deal with it in a creative way?

2. How does a person get out of the cycle of feeling guilty for past failures and receive the forgiveness of God?

3. What "real" situations have you tried to wrestle with? What solutions have you found?

4. Al offers much hope when he says, "If reality has hit you hard recently and you are afraid, alone, or confused, let me encourage you to rely on your faith. Trust that God will give you the grace and wisdom you need. Believe that He has good in store for you." How can your faith help you? What should you do if you are having a hard time believing God?

CHAPTER 11

1. How did Al and Lisa's crisis bring them closer to God? To each other?

2. When the nurse shared with Al about her own premature baby, what effect did that have on him? How does her simple action encourage you to reach out to people with a smile or encouraging word?

3. Romans 5:3–4 and 8:38–39 gave great comfort to Al and Lisa. What promises does God make in these passages? How did they help build character and faith in them?

4. Have you been disappointed by someone who, like the preacher, failed to give you hope, comfort, or encouragement in your hour of greatest need? What lesson did Al learn from this disappointing experience? What can you learn from it as well?

CHAPTER 12

1. Why do you think conflict over money is such a big issue in marriage?

2. What advice would you give to a person who says, "I did not sign up for this"?

3. What do you do when it seems that your spouse or someone you love is blind to how you feel?

4. Lisa writes, "I did not know how to have a healthy, honest conversation with Al about all of this; I just knew I was unhappy." What is the first step in developing the ability to communicate?

CHAPTER 13

1. After reading this chapter, what things would you say are at the root of most unhappy marriages?

2. In what ways is "busyness" an escape from real intimacy?

3. What does the devil try to do in our lives? (See John 10:10.) How does he try to accomplish his purposes?

4. Al pleads, "Have an honest conversation with your spouse, make your needs and desires known, and do your best to work together to reach the level of fulfillment God intends for you to enjoy in marriage." What do you wish you could discuss with your spouse? How are you going to initiate an honest conversation?

CHAPTER 14

1. Why does Lisa refer to secrets as "time bombs"? What should you do if you are trapped by a secret or living a double life?

2. Why is it unwise to reconnect with someone with whom you have had an intimate relationship in the past? Lisa compares this kind of relationship to juggling with what weapon? Why does she use that image?

3. Lisa says, "Something in me drove me to feed the darkness inside me; it kept me keeping secrets and spinning webs of deceit." What does she say was at the root of this bad behavior? Why?

4. Have you ever struggled with the kind of torment Lisa endured—loving Al and not wanting to hurt him, yet hurting him deeply behind his back? If you are in that type of situation, seek help from a qualified therapist who can help you sort

through your feelings before they do even more damage to you or someone you love.

CHAPTER 15

1. Lisa admits to having been a "Christian imposter" for years. What is a "Christian imposter"?

2. How does the way Lisa's friends and support system treated her after the affair became public inspire you to deal with people who may be caught in various kinds of sin or bondage?

3. Why was Lisa's letter to the church so powerful? How do you think that kind of honesty could help a person find healing and restoration?

4. In your own words, what does 1 John 1:9 mean? How did the truth of this verse play out in Lisa's life?

CHAPTER 16

1. What aspects of Al and Lisa's story have most inspired you to believe the best for your own marriage?

2. What role did forgiveness play in Al and Lisa's reconciliation? In a specific situation in your life, whether it's in your marriage or not, how can you extend grace instead of judgment?

3. How are forgiveness and freedom connected?

4. Why did Miss Kay say that Lisa's repentance meant more to her than the repayment of the money Lisa owed Duck Commander? Has anyone ever been that gracious to you? Is there someone in your life to whom you need to extend that kind of grace?

5. Why is honoring and obeying God's Word the pathway to blessing?

CHAPTER 17

1. What motivates Al and Lisa to share their story so honestly and openly?

2. Why is it important to have support from family, friends, and the church when you are having a difficult time?

3. After they reconciled, Al and Lisa were tested. What tests have you experienced? What did you learn?

4. Al says, "The past can be forgiven and redeemed. No matter what has happened, God always offers a second chance . . . I am living proof that second chances exist." What in your past needs to be forgiven and redeemed?

CHAPTER 18

1. Why is it important to learn to look at life in terms of seasons, realizing that everything on earth is temporary?

2. If you are going through a difficult time right now, how does reading about Al and Lisa's life today give you hope for your future?

3. Al writes: "The salvation we received from Christ was our first step to a better life, a better way of thinking, and a better way of handling the effects of sin and its consequences." How have you seen that through their story in this book?

4. Will you believe that, no matter what you are going through, God can heal and redeem every aspect of brokenness you have ever experienced in your life? What difference will believing this make in your life?

5. What do the following Bible verses mean to you personally? John 3:16, Romans 8:8–10, Romans 6:1–14, Galatians 5:16–26.

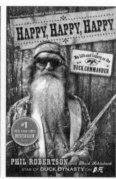

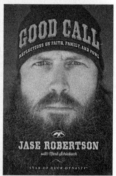

Get email updates on

AL ROBERTSON,

exclusive offers, and other great book recommendations from Simon & Schuster.

Visit **newsletters.simonandschuster.com**

or scan below to sign up:

Get email updates on

LISA ROBERTSON,

exclusive offers, and other great book recommendations from Simon & Schuster.

Visit **newsletters.simonandschuster.com**

or scan below to sign up: